TOWARDS A HUMANE REFUGEE POLICY FOR THE EUROPEAN UNION

The Foundation for European Progressive Studies (FEPS) is the think tank of the progressive political family at EU level. Our mission is to develop innovative research, policy advice, training and debates to inspire and inform progressive politics and policies across Europe. We operate as hub for thinking to facilitate the emergence of progressive answers to the challenges that Europe faces today.

FEPS works in close partnership with its members and partners, forging connections and boosting coherence among stakeholders from the world of politics, academia and civil society at local, regional, national, European and global levels.

Today FEPS benefits from a solid network of 71 member organisations. Among these, 40 are full members, 26 have observer status and 5 are ex-officio members. In addition to this network of organisations that are active in the promotion of progressive values, FEPS also has an extensive network of partners, including renowned universities, scholars, policymakers and activists.

Our ambition is to undertake intellectual reflection for the benefit of the progressive movement, and to promote the founding principles of the EU – freedom, equality, solidarity, democracy, respect of human rights, fundamental freedoms and human dignity, and respect of the rule of law.

TOWARDS A HUMANE REFUGEE POLICY FOR THE EUROPEAN UNION

Gesine Schwan
with the collaboration of Malisa Zobel

Book published in June 2023 by the Foundation for European Progressive Studies in association with London Publishing Partnership

Originally published as "Europa versagt. Eine menschliche Flüchtlingspolitik ist möglich" by Gesine Schwan. Copyright © 2021 S. Fischer Verlag GmbH, Frankfurt am Main

A catalogue record for this book is available from the British Library

FOUNDATION FOR EUROPEAN PROGRESSIVE STUDIES (FEPS)

Avenue des Arts 46 – 1000 Brussels, Belgium
www.feps-europe.eu
@FEPS_Europe

Supervision: Hedwig Giusto
Layout and editing: T&T Productions Ltd, London
Cover photograph: Adobe Stock

This book was published with the financial support of the European Parliament. It does not represent the view of the European Parliament.

ISBN: 978-1-913019-91-4 (pbk)
ISBN: 978-1-913019-92-1 (ePDF)
ISBN: 978-1-913019-93-8 (ePUB)

Table of contents

Preface

Europe's refugee policy is deeply troubling to many and in particular to committed Europeans. With courage and a willingness to make sacrifices, they are fighting against inhumanity – by taking part in sea rescues and through numerous civic initiatives, in cities and municipalities, in companies, in churches, in academia and also in political parties, parliaments and associations. Were it not for the complex mix of party-political power struggles and sensationalist media campaigns, our European societies would have found more humane solutions long ago.

We must escape this deadlock of inhumanity as quickly as we can. This book aims to highlight how this can be done. I am convinced that our values and our legitimate long-term interests intersect and reinforce each other.

I would particularly like to thank my colleague Dr Malisa Zobel for her long, close collaboration on this topic and on the manuscript – in agreement on the objective but not always on the individual steps required to achieve it. I was always touched and encouraged by her persistent persuasiveness, which I found delightful. In this book, she wrote the sections on the "right of asylum in the European Union", on the proposal for a "matching system" to coordinate the interests of refugees and municipalities, and on the concept of "decentralised asylum procedures in individual European nation states". Furthermore, she carefully reviewed and corrected the entire manuscript.

I would also like to express my enormous gratitude to the Schöpflin Foundation: to the committed and unconventional philanthropist Hans Schöpflin, with his generous support for the HUMBOLDT-VIADRINA Governance Platform's refugee project; to project manager Anna Hässlin, who provides critical guidance and support with exceptional astuteness; and to CEO Tim Göbel, who keeps a watchful eye over every aspect of its finances.

I am also very grateful to Dr Steffen Angenendt, who took the time to go through the manuscript and furnish it with many valuable comments, questions and objections. Gerald Knaus, who knows the numbers of refugees and migrants better than anyone else, provided me with very useful documents that enabled me to estimate the numbers of refugees and migrants living in undignified and, in some cases, clearly illegal conditions in the Balkans and on the Greek islands. I am extremely grateful for his assistance. I would also like to thank in particular the SPD members of the Bundestag Professor Dr Lars Castellucci and Helge Lindh, as well as the Social Democratic Members of the European Parliament (MEPs) Udo Bullmann and Jens Geier, who are unwavering in their commitment to fighting for a humane refugee policy. Without their close collaboration and that of other members of the Group of Socialists and Democrats in the European Parliament, I would have missed out on many valuable insights; time and again, they helped me to reconcile political realism and ethical intransigence.

The former chair of the Group of Socialists and Democrats Maria João Rodrigues, who hails from Portugal, provided me with the idea of a financial incentive for the admission of refugees, initially conceived as a way to support states that wish to admit refugees and that, in particular, need to create jobs for them in order to be able to do so.

As president of the Foundation for European Progressive Studies (FEPS), Maria João Rodrigues – together with the EU High Representative of the Union for Foreign Affairs and Security Policy, Josep Borell, and the secretary general of FEPS, László Andor – ensured that the basic idea of the strategy outlined in the book (the strengthening of municipalities' role in admitting refugees) played an important part in the 2018 Global Compact for Safe, Orderly and Regular Migration.

The current vice president of the European Parliament, Dr Katarina Barley, is a tireless campaigner for the humane refugee policy outlined here. I am enormously grateful to her for her efforts in this regard. Dr Franziska Brandtner, member of the Bundestag for Bündnis90/Die Grünen and parliamentary state secretary in the federal ministry of economics and climate protection, and the late Dr Axel Troost, who was a member of the Bundestag for Die Linke (and of the party's federal executive committee), have been important figures in the pursuit of a humane refugee policy. I am also grateful to them.

The German Trade Union Confederation was also very helpful, along with its former president Reiner Hoffmann, who included the outline of the strategy in his 2019 election programme for the European Parliament.

The Friedrich Ebert Stiftung EU Office took up the strategy proposed here in the form of conferences during Renate Tenbusch's term as its head. Marco Funk and his successor, Tobias Schmitt, who were responsible for the topic in Brussels, have played their part in implementing a humane refugee policy and continue to do so today. My heartfelt thanks go out to all three of them for their efforts!

For having promoted this strategy to President Emmanuel Macron, I am hugely indebted and grateful to the French ambassador in Berlin, Anne-Marie Descôtes; her predecessors Philippe Étienne and Maurice Gourdault-Montagne; and the Green MEP Daniel Cohn-Bendit. Macron's promotion of the core idea of a "European Fund for Municipal Integration and Development" to the European Parliament in spring 2017 was of enormous significance.

Dr Marek Prawda, ambassador in Berlin and Brussels for many years and, until recently, head of the European Commission's Representation in Warsaw, has been consistently and unwaveringly committed to a humane refugee policy in Europe, and in Poland in particular, despite the adverse political conditions. This is also true of Róża Thun, a Polish MEP, and her husband, Franz Thun, who was responsible for this topic in the administration of Poland's capital, Warsaw, and of Professor Dr Irena Lipowicz, long-time ombudswoman of the pre-PiS Polish government and professor of administrative law, who is committed to the aim of strengthening municipalities. In Gdańsk, Marta Siciarek displayed her long-standing commitment to the humane reception of refugees for many years under the city's courageous mayor Pawel Adamowicz, who was assassinated in 2019, and she continues to do so to this day. I am deeply indebted to them all.

In the winter of 2020, Jörg Bong became instantly enthusiastic about this book project and persuaded Fischer Verlag to publish the original German edition. I am enormously grateful to him.

Finally, I would like to extend my sincerest thanks to Ulrike Holler and Dr Alexander Roesler for their involvement, encouragement and support for this book from very outset.

Introduction

On 20 July 1957 my French friend Claudette Caze and I watched the Polish film *Ostatni Etap* (*The Last Stage*) in the Free University of Berlin's Auditorium Maximum. We were both 14 years old. The Polish director, Wanda Jakubowska, had made the film as a dramatised document of Auschwitz, where she herself had been interned from 1942 until the camp's evacuation in 1945. I was greatly moved and shocked by the film, which permanently shaped my political beliefs. I was unable to sleep at all that night. In my mind was the scene in which hundreds of prisoners were forced to spend the night standing in temperatures of minus 20 degrees Celsius in the courtyard of Auschwitz. They pressed close together and swayed slightly – rhythmically back and forth – in an attempt to survive this ordeal together.

A few years later I learned of the fate of the ship the *St Louis*. Following the 1938 *Kristallnacht* pogrom, 937 Jewish Germans were trying to emigrate from Hamburg to Cuba and the United States on this ship, which was owned by the Hapag shipping company. Most of them had the necessary documentation to do so. However, with the exception of a few passengers in Cuba, they were not allowed to disembark. The ship's German captain, Gustav Schröder, personally asked President Roosevelt to allow the passengers to enter the United States. His request was in vain. The president, who at first wished to grant permission, bowed to pressure from his party, the Democrats, sections of which threatened to withdraw their support for him in the 1940 presidential election if he allowed the Jewish refugees to land. The Canadian prime minister also refused to let the passengers disembark. The ship was forced to return to Europe; it was finally given permission to land in Belgium, and from Antwerp the passengers were dispersed to the Netherlands, France and Britain. Only those accepted by Britain were safe, even if they were interned. For all the others, a terrifying and often fatal odyssey awaited them. According to research conducted by the United States Holocaust Memorial Museum, 254 passengers were eventually murdered in the Holocaust.

In 2012 the US State Department apologised to ten surviving passengers of the *St Louis*. Six years later Canada's prime minister, Justin Trudeau, said to applause in the country's national parliament, "We are sorry for the callousness of Canada's response," adding: "We refused to help them when we could have. We contributed to sealing the cruel fates of far too many at places like Auschwitz, Treblinka, and Belzec."[1]

My recollections of these two events continue to drive me to remain unrelenting in the attempt to find a humane approach to receiving refugees in Europe. There are, of course, many other moral and political motives and considerations, but the bitter historical experience that democratic politicians succumbed to the unspeakably inhumane pressure from parts of their society, their parties and their voters to not admit the fleeing Jews – despite the deadly threat from the Nazis – is something that I find particularly shameful and an inescapable mandate to do everything possible to ensure that such things never occur again. If the binding ethical and legal standards to which we democrats publicly commit ourselves are disregarded, even in democracies where there are no physical threats, any failure to act makes us complicit.

A pragmatic and humane response to the challenges posed by the refugee protection crisis is most likely to be found in municipalities and their active civil society, which is why the role they play is pivotal. The proposals I outline below are by no means the only panacea for EU migration and refugee policy. The complexities of the politics surrounding refugees and asylum seekers make it impossible for one book to solve all the problems, and this is particularly true for the EU's policies, which are marked by tensions that extend far beyond migration and refugee issues. These proposals are, though, an attempt to present an alternative to the current inhumane isolationist policy.

*

This book deals only with European refugee policy. While it also looks at Africa and the Middle East, it is unable to cover the global dimension of migration. I am aware that the problems in other parts of the world are just as pressing.

---

1   Trudeau, J. (2018) "Statement of apology on behalf of the Government of Canada to the passengers of the MS St. Louis". Website of the Prime Minister of Canada, 7 November (https://pm.gc.ca/en/news/speeches/2018/11/07/statement-apology-behalf-government-canada-passengers-ms-st-louis).

When talking about Europe, I am referring to the EU's most important political actors in the area of migration policy. These are the European Commission, the European Parliament, the European External Action Service and, most importantly, the European Council (the heads of state or government of the EU member states). The European Border and Coast Guard Agency (Frontex) and the European Union Agency for Asylum are responsible for the executive functions.

The key propositions of this book in brief

- The European Union's refugee policy is failing because its actions are contrary to the values it proclaims.

- This ethical contradiction harms us all as Europeans. We are losing credibility and trust both internally and externally, and we are destroying our social and political cohesion along with the basis on which our democracies are built. We are squandering the opportunities for a rich, constructive and meaningful common future, both at home and in the global North–South relationship.

- If we are to achieve a humane refugee policy, we must abandon the guiding principle of current European refugee policy – which is to deter refugees wherever possible – in favour of the realisation that it is possible to shape refugee policy as a win-win strategy that accords with our own long-term interests.

- The practical way to break the deadlock around the current refugee policy is to reach a voluntary agreement on the acceptance of refugees in a coalition of willing states and to offer positive encouragement, including the use of financial incentives, instead of obliging all EU states to "accept" refugees under the threat of sanctions. Voluntary agreement turns refugees into an opportunity rather than a burden.

- When it comes to refugee policy, aligning long-term interests and values is easiest at the municipal level, where the two can be coordinated transparently and with the approval of citizens. A humane refugee policy could also be combined with a successful extension of effective civic engagement in line with the principles of representative democracy. That too is an advantage.

- In line with the UN Sustainable Development Goals for 2030 and with long-term municipal integration and development, "municipal development councils" could integrate the reception of refugees into their future planning for their municipalities. Willing states could cooperate with willing municipalities to distribute refugees to the various municipalities. A matching system could align the interests of refugees with those of municipalities.

- The funding for their reception could be provided by a "European Fund for Municipal Integration and Development", which would make it easy for municipalities that are willing to receive refugees to apply for funding for refugee integration and to also receive the same amount of funding for projects that are in their own interest.

- Humane asylum procedures require transparency, fairness, trustworthiness and swiftness. Legal support and the presence of organised civil society are crucial factors in asylum procedures. Different categories of refugees require complementary immigration and employment arrangements.

- Humane asylum procedures can be conducted in centralised European assessment centres or at the national level.

- Refugees with the right to asylum, those with subsidiary protection and those who cannot be returned ("tolerated stay") should be treated equally by the matching procedure. Those who clearly have no right to asylum and are unable to transfer to alternative and possibly temporary residence programmes must be returned to their countries of origin, where possible with financial support.

- Concerns about a pull factor for refugees, from Africa in particular, can be overcome only by a change of perspective and by taking a fresh look at Europe's diverse neighbouring continent. Instead of an attempt to maintain an illusory and inhumane isolation for Europe, a cooperative partnership that accords with the long-term interests of Europe and Africa offers both sides opportunities for positive development in line with their respective long-term legitimate interests.

- In both Europe and Africa, municipalities and the European Committee of the Regions can play an important constructive role.

A "business as usual" approach to refugee policy is not only shameful and inhumane but also a threat to Europe's future, democracy and peace. It detracts from the sense of purpose and the joy from understanding and harmonious coexistence in Europe and beyond.

1 | The scandal of Fortress Europe: EU refugee policy contravenes European values and international law

1.1 Is the European Union on the right track?

Europe, both in the form of the European Union and as a political model, continues to benefit from a positive reputation despite the multiple crises in its history. These crises, however, did ultimately result in increased cohesion, and Europe now attracts many people from all over the world. It embodies a wealth of traditions and a diverse culture, and it is seen as offering people a future in which they can express their individuality while enjoying social security, responsibility and solidarity. For centuries, Europe endured brutal wars and political excesses, but in an extraordinary and admirable turn of events it seemed to have finally learned its lesson after World War II: an end to wars, nationalism and domestic conflicts – instead, peace at home and abroad, freedom, and political and social responsibility. Those were the lessons learned in the aftermath of Nazism and the war. The fall of communism in 1989 offered the opportunity to finally extend this promise far beyond Western Europe. This historical ability to learn from past mistakes was and is a unique asset of the European Union.

In 1989 many believed that an age of freedom, peace and democracy had dawned for the entire world. Some, like Francis Fukuyama, hubristically declared that history had come to an end with the definitive victory of liberal democracies. More prudent minds understood that history never ends and that democracies need to work tirelessly on their internal consolidation and stabilisation. Nonetheless, everything seemed to be on the right track, even if it was a long one.

The current situation looks very different. Liberal democracies around the world are being challenged by authoritarian and even autocratic regimes and radical right-wing parties; the former conflict between East and West blocs has potentially restarted with Putin's attack on Ukraine, in the form of a polarisation between democracies and authoritarian or autocratic regimes; and traditional wars between nation states have mostly been replaced by innumerable civil wars. Western liberal societies are embroiled in destructive internal strife. The gulf between the rich and poor is getting ever wider. These divisions have not only social and political consequences but also economic ones, and these are giving rise to new global crises, particularly in the financial markets.

While US democracy has long been held up as exemplary, the presidency of Donald Trump has shown that the indispensable institutions of democracy alone are not enough: the ultimate cornerstone of freedom, democracy and peace lies in the attitude of the citizenry. The history of European and American ideas provides many observations and justifications of this principle, not least Madison's emphasis on the "people" in the 57th Article of the Federalist Papers, the fundamental treatise on the US Constitution:

> If it be asked, what is to restrain the House of Representatives from making legal discriminations in favour of themselves and a particular class of the society? I answer: the genius of the whole system; the nature of just and constitutional laws; and above all, the vigilant and manly spirit which actuates the people of America, a spirit which nourishes freedom, and in return is nourished by it.[1]

If we now move from the United States to the global arena, we see that multipolarity has replaced East–West conflict. This encourages the antagonistic politics that prevailed in the 19th century and led to the catastrophe of World War I. Instead of a policy of peace based on a multilateral understanding between states and on stabilising treaties, the world faces the threat of a new spiral of deterrence, armament, mutual mistrust, ruthlessness, vituperative polemics and boastful grandstanding. Power is supplanting law in many states, brazen lies are replacing a belief in facts and a common search for truth, and natural disasters dominate the global news, evoking dystopias rather than utopias and instilling fear instead of confidence. The outlook is not good for the founding objectives of the European Union: peace, freedom, prosperity and human rights. This is also reflected in the fact that the EU has initiated a rule-of-law procedure (under Article 7 of the Treaty on European Union) against Poland and Hungary to determine whether they are violating the

---

1   Hamilton, A., J. Madison and J. Jay (2009) *The Federalist Papers* (Newhaven, CT: Yale University Press).

fundamental values of the European Union. Viktor Orbán, Hungary's long-time head of government, has openly turned away from liberal democracy and embraced "illiberal democracy". In addition, the Covid-19 pandemic kept the world on tenterhooks from spring 2020, with enormously varied and unpredictable consequences.

Unlike the financial crisis, the economic slump in the EU that accompanied the pandemic has resulted in a revival of the solidarity between the economically poorer states and their richer counterparts (a solidarity that had deteriorated over the years) in the form of a joint credit-financed reconstruction fund. Before the crisis, such an economically sensible response had always failed because of the richer states, in particular Germany.

Some of the more important reasons for this seismic change in favour of European solidarity and economic cooperation were that the economic collapse was caused by the Covid-19 pandemic (and thus could not be put down to the "moral failings" of national governments and societies, as happened during the sovereign debt crisis); that the decision of Germany's chancellor not to stand in the 2021 Bundestag election allowed her to act in a nonpartisan manner; and that the German finance minister, Olaf Scholz, was able to convince the stronger, exporting countries to support the weaker ones on the basis of their own long-term interest of preserving their European sales markets, and to thus put aside earlier ideological fixations.

Furthermore, the increasingly ominous natural disasters reported daily and vividly in the media, as well as the dynamic Fridays for Future movement, are causing a profound shift in consciousness and public sentiment that can benefit sustainable policies in the EU. This shift is currently focused primarily on the environmental and climate-related facets of sustainability, but the social and economic causes and consequences of climate change are becoming ever more tangible, increasing the urgency of comprehensive policies that encompass sustainability's social aspects. Politics can no longer be simply about tactical power plays with an eye on the next general election. Instead it must take into account all the long-term risks and consequences of its decisions. Despite this insight, accurately identifying and assessing those risks and consequences and incorporating them into policymaking will continue to be a complex challenge. Success will require developing and safeguarding transparency, the rule of law and the greatest possible degree of carefully conceived democratic participation.

1.2 The scandal of European refugee and asylum policy

The European Union could be well on the way to achieving its aims were it not for the enormous scandal of its asylum and refugee policy. This policy attests to deeper-seated contradictions within the EU: does the EU see itself as a community of values, characterised by intra-European solidarity, or as a loose community of states, in which national self-interests prevail over European ones? The more conservative the national governments are, the more pronounced their national focus and the less they prioritise European solidarity.

The EU's refugee policy not only makes a mockery of its values and its obligations under human rights conventions and international law: the day-to-day contradiction between its proclaimed values and its actions, which can only be described as cynical, is also destroying the EU's future, its democratic cohesion, and the way of life that it stands for and that its citizens expect. The EU has no long-term future if it lacks an active and credible global policy that promotes peace, freedom, justice and solidarity for all people. It also needs a convincing commitment to the welfare of all. It is inevitable that those who consistently betray their own values and human rights commitments in important areas of external policy will eventually do so domestically too, as can already be clearly seen in Hungary and Poland. Such a betrayal also leads to the destruction of any protections against the subversion of democracy – protections that democracy needs to ensure its survival, as the Federalist Papers have shown.

Today's political systems – democratic ones in particular – are challenged by ever higher levels of education, global interdependence, the dynamics of unrestrained capitalism, instant access to information and constantly evolving technology. If we fail to shape those factors, they will come to dominate us. Political systems can no longer survive as either instruments of oppression or laissez-faire structures, or by simply drifting in an unstable manner. Neither governmental manipulation of communications and exclusive reliance on consumer interests nor political repression is a sustainable political model, despite the propagandistic claims of the authoritarian and sometimes clearly dictatorial regimes that seem to be on the rise, such as in Hungary or, until recently, Brazil. In the long run, people will not put up with being deprived of freedom, justice and meaning in their lives, not even under a political system such as China's. If political systems are not to eventually descend into state-perpetrated violence or civil war, they need not only the voluntary consent of the population but also their participation, drive and capacity to solve problems. These are indispensable if the people are to feel invested in the political system despite its manifold political conflicts.

What events have occurred in asylum and refugee policy in the European Union in recent years? In September 2015 the German chancellor, Angela Merkel, did not want to close the German borders to refugees from Syria and elsewhere in the Middle East who were fleeing the conflict in the region. In view of the worsening humanitarian conditions for those trekking across the Balkans, the chancellor decided – after consulting with the Austrian chancellor – to not exacerbate the emergency any further and to permit the refugees to cross the border. This did not in any way violate the applicable regulations, as the Dublin III Regulation determines which member state is responsible for the asylum procedure only in principle, and a country can at any time decide to assume that responsibility on its own initiative. An important fact to bear in mind when assessing the German chancellor's decision is that she did not *open* the borders – instead, she decided not to close them. If she had reacted differently and Germany, like Hungary, had refused political responsibility for the arriving people, she would most likely have triggered a fierce international reaction, which was one thing she wanted to avoid.

However, her decision was an in-the-moment reaction to a particular situation and not the result of a well-conceived, long-term refugee policy. Indeed, it was only a few weeks later that she replaced the policy with one whose effective aim was to ensure that refugees were kept out of Germany and the EU. But despite this, Merkel maintained her humanitarian rhetoric. Since then there has been a lack of direction in Germany and among the other European heads of government about the objectives and possibilities of a European asylum and refugee policy; there is a vacillation between theoretical values and practical cynicism. "I have been working with refugees for over three decades. But in those three decades I have never seen such toxicity, such poisonous language in politics, media and social media, even in everyday discussions and conversations around this issue as I do today," says Filippo Grandi, the UN High Commissioner for Refugees.[2]

---

2   "Filippo Grandi (UNHCR) on the briefing by the United Nations High Commissioner for Refugees – Security Council, 8504th meeting". *UN Web TV*, 9 April 2019 (https://media.un.org/en/asset/k1c/k1cjiwqnde).

The Council of Europe's Commissioner for Human Rights, Dunja Mija-tović, makes serious accusations in her March 2021 report on EU refugee policy, in which she states that EU migration policy causes "thousands of avoidable deaths" in the Mediterranean each year. The European countries have engaged in a "race to the bottom" to keep "people in need of protection outside our borders – with terrible consequences".[3] That is the balance sheet since 2015.

The only thing the governments of the European Council all agree on is their demand for "better protection of the external borders" in order to prevent as many refugees as possible – and, for some governments, any refugees at all – from entering Europe. Officially, this falls under the slogan of stopping "illegal migration". This suggests that refugees and migrants have the option of legal migration or legal access routes to the EU, which is only sporadically the case, in the form of so-called resettlement programmes. The absence of legal access routes is primarily due to airlines' strict conditions of carriage and highly restrictive visa policies. Most citizens of countries outside the Organisation for Economic Co-operation and Development are unable to enter the Schengen area without a valid visa. It is almost impossible for those claiming asylum from war or political persecution on the basis of certain characteristics to obtain a visa for the Schengen area.[4] Even the idea of humanitarian visas, supported by the European Parliament,[5] has not been put into practice. This means that most of those claiming asylum do not have a valid visa and have to attempt to enter the European Union illicitly. Even the much-defended theoretical right of an individual to have their claim to protection examined is an empty one if there is no legal access to the means of exercising it in the EU. In reality, the heads of state and government are actively working to prevent this right from being exercised.

---

3   Zick, T. (2021) "Schwere Vorwürfe gegen Europas Flüchtlingspolitik". *Süddeutsche Zeitung*, 9 March (www.sueddeutsche.de/politik/migration-mittelmeer-europa-menschen rechte-1.5229226).

4   In war zones, particularly during civil wars, there are few or no functioning embassies where one could apply for a visa; even where they do exist, applicants face long waiting times, and time is something that politically persecuted people do not have.

5   "Humanitarian visas: 'A right to be heard without risking your life'". European Parliament website, 6 December 2018 (www.europarl.europa.eu/news/en/headlines/wor ld/20181031STO18177/humanitarian-visas-a-right-to-be-heard-without-risking-your-life).

1.3 The attempt to Europeanise European asylum and refugee policy

The European Union has been trying to agree on a common asylum policy since the 1990s, so far without success. To date, it has failed to agree on a fair "distribution" system between the member states for receiving, accommodating and caring for asylum seekers and examining their claims to protection. Even the term "distribution" reveals one of the reasons for this failure. It implies that refugees can be distributed like so much cargo, and that Europe's refugee policy is based on the interests of nation states rather than the rights of refugees.

The abolition of internal borders through the Schengen Agreement and the simultaneous increase (due to the wars in the former Yugoslavia) in the number of asylum seekers, especially in Germany, led to the implementation of the Dublin Convention in 1997. The convention, which was incorporated into the Dublin III Regulation, continues to determine which country is responsible for examining a claim for protection (the asylum procedure). As a rule, the country responsible is the first EU state entered. The Dublin Regulation was of importance, first and foremost, to Germany, and following the EU's eastern enlargement in 2004 it meant that asylum seekers hoping to enter Germany would need to do so by air or via the North Sea, because in all other instances other EU countries lay between Germany and the EU's external borders. Because access to asylum procedures was now possible only in the EU's external border states, they theoretically bore sole responsibility for receiving, accommodating and caring for asylum seekers, and also for examining their claims for protection. Given this obvious injustice, in practice the external states simply let the refugees move north without registering them.

The prevailing political view in Germany was that asylum seekers were a burden and should be excluded wherever possible, and it was on this basis that Germany had, in effect, used EU law to "secure" itself against refugees. A clear indication of this fundamental attitude is that interior ministers have consistently proclaimed their successes in asylum and refugee policy in terms of reductions in refugees entering the country or increases in refugees being deported. This attitude has remained unchanged and even become more entrenched over the years in German government policy and in the European Council, the body that ultimately decides European asylum policy. It is a premise held, of course, by conservative governments, but also, for example, by the leader of Denmark's social democratic government, who, since spring 2021, has even wanted to deport Syrians and to force them into deportation camps in the interim.[6] It is linked to the unspoken assumption that displacement and migration are exceptional situations, that EU-wide solutions are not required and that the challenges can safely be ignored. This view clearly contradicts the values the EU proclaims to hold. It is also a direct consequence of the fact that the EU's need for a common asylum and refugee policy, rather than purely national regulations, came about not because of humanitarian motives but instead from its desire to secure national borders. Following the implementation of the Schengen Agreement and the opening up of the EU's internal borders, focus shifted to its external frontiers. Refugee policy thus became the responsibility of interior ministers, and asylum seekers were perceived primarily from the perspective of a risk to borders, external security and state sovereignty. Defence and national security were therefore very much at the forefront when asylum and refugee policy was being formulated.

This political perspective arose partly from a traditional scepticism and even hostility towards foreigners, which, for centuries, has meant that the equally traditional sense of the moral virtue of granting asylum and protection from persecution has had to be defended. This debate, a familiar topic in academia, has intensified in the European public sphere since the sharp increase in the numbers of arriving asylum seekers in 2015 and 2016. In previous years, the countries at the forefront – Greece, Italy and Spain – repeatedly demanded solidarity from their European neighbours because of the high number of asylum seekers arriving at their borders, but those neighbours turned a deaf ear, including Germany under Chancellor Merkel. Only when the southern countries began "waving through" the hundreds of thousands of people arriving and let them travel on north, in the summer of 2015, did those neighbours start to address the challenge. The asylum seekers had fled in large numbers from the Syrian civil war, and from the refugee camps in Lebanon, which offered few prospects for a better future. Those already poor prospects in the camps were then further worsened when the United Nations High Commissioner for Refugees (UNHCR) was forced to cut its grants by 50% as a result of UN member states – including Germany – greatly reducing or halting their payments. The reduction in payments shows how little

---

6 Strittmatter, K. (2021) "Dänemark schickt Geflüchtete zurück nach Syrien". *Süddeutsche Zeitung*, 15 April (www.sueddeutsche.de/politik/daenemark-syrien-asyl-fluechtlinge-1.5265844).

heed the EU countries had paid prior to 2015 to the political challenge of refugee policy as a long-term endeavour.

In September 2015, at a time when a rapidly increasing number of asylum seekers were stuck in Budapest, Germany's chancellor, Angela Merkel, consulted with Austria's chancellor, Werner Faymann, and then issued assurances that Germany's borders would remain open for asylum seekers in Hungary to travel on to Austria and Germany. In 2015 a total of around 900,000 refugees arrived in Germany this way and were not initially registered.

This period is seen by many observers as a turning point in European and German asylum and refugee policy, because the external border states were no longer able to cope with the number of arrivals and therefore stopped registering people. This then officially called into question the existing Dublin Convention, which explicitly assigned responsibility to the external border states. In addition, the reform of the Common European Asylum System and the Dublin Regulation – a reform that the European Parliament had already agreed on – became bogged down in the European Council. The current state of limbo has now persisted for several years, and many, including the German chancellor, now consider the Dublin Convention (in the form of the Dublin III Regulation), which is still formally applicable, to be outdated and no longer practicable, because Dublin III neither includes solidarity with the main countries of arrival nor effectively regulates the "relocation" of refugees. However, agreement on a new regulation on access to asylum procedures has yet to be found.

Even the European Commission's much-heralded new draft of September 2020 does not address the issues of securing access to the asylum process and the relocation of refugees. The focus is clearly on shutting Europe's external borders even more firmly, on turning away asylum seekers from outside the EU wherever possible and on either blackmailing or bribing the African states to work in the interests of the EU by turning away refugees or taking back those who are deported. Of course, this is not stated in such explicit terms but instead camouflaged in humanitarian language. In addition, the new Commission proposal exempts the EU states from the previous "imposition" of admitting asylum seekers on the basis of solidarity, but it sets out no discernible alternative proposal for any system of incentives to admit them. At the same time, it continues to maintain the fiction of a pan-European asylum policy. It is impossible to imagine a more radical de facto renunciation of a common European asylum and refugee policy than this contradiction between rhetoric and practice.

As a result, the European Union has not managed to initiate or implement an asylum and refugee policy that even comes close to meeting the standards it is supposedly committed to maintaining. On the contrary, the EU is increasingly reliant on the Libyan coastguard, which is allowing refugees to drown or illicitly returning them to Libya, and the EU is thus in reality supporting the maintenance of camps in Libya where human rights are violated through torture and rape. In its actual practice – with the camps on Lesbos, Chios and Lipa; with thousands dead in the Mediterranean and recently also in the Atlantic; with ever more frequent "refoulements" in the Mediterranean and on the Balkan route, in violation of international law; and with unknown numbers dying of thirst in the Sahara – the European Union is constantly acting in contradiction to its assertions of the values that supposedly guide its policies. Despite this, nothing changes.

Before the Moria camp on Lesbos was destroyed by fire, UN High Commissioner for Refugees Filippo Grandi visited it and, according to a report by Deutsche Welle, condemned the conditions there, saying that he found the situation to be unacceptable, with violence and exploitation commonplace. Christos Christou, head of the Greek branch of Doctors Without Borders, considered the situation in Moria to be a "normalisation and justification of misery".[7]

The catastrophic situation in the camps on the Greek islands has deteriorated over time. In 2015 the EU launched a relocation programme to enable 160,000 asylum seekers to move from Greece and Italy to other member states. In reality, only a fraction of the 160,000 were given the chance to do so. Germany, for example, had promised to accept some 27,000 people, but only about a third of them were ever actually admitted. Although everyone in Europe knew that the camps on the Greek islands were overcrowded, the European governments refused to take in sick people and unaccompanied children in any significant numbers until Christmas 2020. The German government always has two standard justifications for this: it does not wish to act unilaterally within the EU and it does not want to trigger a pull effect. I will return to both of these "justifications" later.

One of the most recent cases of European inhumanity was the treatment of refugees from the burnt-down camp of Lipa, in northern Bosnia. Friedrich Merz – who had just lost the run-off election for chair of the Christian Democratic Union, yet who nevertheless represented a

---

7 "UN geißeln Bedingungen in griechischen Flüchtlingslagern". *Deutsche Welle*, 27 November 2019 (www.dw.com/de/un-geißeln-bedingungen-in-griechischen-flüchtling slagern/a-51442802).

considerable portion of the party's members – refused to let the refugees who were being shunted back and forth come to Germany. He justified his position with the remark: "This humanitarian catastrophe cannot be solved by us saying, 'Come to Germany, all of you.' That approach is no longer an option."[8] He omits to mention that this approach was never "an option", that it was never the case that "all" refugees came to Germany, that in fact the vast majority of displaced persons generally remain close to home in their own country or within the African continent.

Nor does he press for solutions. With regard to the unresolved question of rescues at sea, Merz came up with nothing more than the following response: "The best thing would be for these people not to set sail at all." (Ibid.) The best thing would be if there were no refugees …

The UN High Commissioner for Refugees is "slowly losing patience" with the lack of initiative and courage among European politicians:

> To be honest, […] every time European politicians meet and talk about refugee policy, not much good comes out of it. There doesn't even need to be a crisis. Many politicians' fear of the refugee issue has become blown out of all proportion. Angela Merkel seems to me to be the one still acting with the most common sense. Other politicians are almost paranoid.
>
> Last week we had to ask the Ugandan government to take in tens of thousands of displaced people from Congo. Uganda has enough problems of its own, yet its government agreed to do so. If Uganda can do it, why can't Europe? One of the richest places on earth is failing to get its act together. I am slowly losing patience.[9]

In her video message on the occasion of the 20th Berlin Symposium on Refugee Rights, the Council of Europe's Commissioner for Human Rights, Dunja Mijatović (from Bosnia and Herzegovina), criticised and condemned the refugee policies of the members of the Council of Europe, many of which are also members of the EU:

> Increasingly, when designing asylum and migration policies, the focus of member states does not seem to be on ensuring compliance with the Convention [the European

---

8 "'Cannot be the solution': Merz's reaction to receiving refugees from Bosnia and Greece". *Frankfurter Rundschau*, 2 January 2021 (www.fr.de/politik/friedrich-merz-cdu-aufnahme-fluechtlinge-bosnien-griechenland-90156943.html).

9 Lüdke, S. (2020) "UNHCR head on EU refugee policy: 'One of the richest places on earth is failing to get its act together'". *Der Spiegel*, 30 June (www.spiegel.de/ausland/un hcr-chef-filippo-grandi-ueber-fluechtlinge-wenn-uganda-das-schafft-warum-nicht-europa -a-ad9a28b5-3204-4fb2-a733-973c3c698e77).

Convention on Human Rights]. Rather, the focus is on finding new ways to prevent such obligations from becoming applicable in the first place. [...]

This is particularly evident in the Mediterranean. When the Court [the European Court of Human Rights] found, in the Hirsi Jamaa case, that the interception and return of migrants to Libya violated Article 3 of the Convention, it gave a clear signal to member states. Although direct returns to Libya largely stopped, the Hirsi Jamaa judgment has been used as a blueprint to develop new practices to try and avoid effective control of those at sea. This has included outsourcing rescue to the Libyan authorities, without any human rights safeguards in place. While this puts Council of Europe member states at arms' length from events, it does nothing to stop people from being exposed to torture or inhuman or degrading treatment. Even if member states argue that this conforms to the letter of the Convention, a matter that remains to be seen, I believe this approach is hugely damaging to its spirit.

[...] Years and sometimes decades of inadequate implementation and lack of investment in reception and asylum systems have transformed a manageable issue into political chaos. Strong anti-migrant rhetoric is on the increase in many European countries, including in regions where very few or no migrants have settled. The Court has been clear that states have the right to control their borders, but this must be done in compliance with obligations under the Convention. However, politicians increasingly feed the suggestion that human rights are not an essential element of border control, but a hindrance to it. And that human rights must thus be sacrificed for the sake of protecting national or European borders. This narrative has an important European dimension. It is not rare for government officials from one member state to implicitly condone unlawful practices, such as pushbacks, in another. Or even to explicitly praise states for carrying these out.[10]

These two statements, one from a UN official charged with promoting human rights and the other from an official at the Council of Europe, succinctly summarise numerous, amply documented violations of human rights and international law by the European Union. They also expose the logic of the EU's asylum and refugee policy, which increasingly blatantly and systematically disregards international law and human rights. If this way of thinking is not overcome, we will betray the responsibility imposed on us by the historical crimes of the 20th century and also wreck peace, freedom, well-being and the norms on which our democratic political coexistence is based.

---

10   Mijatović, D. (2020) "Protecting refugees in Europe: the ECHR and beyond". Council of Europe, 22 June (https://rm.coe.int/protecting-refugees-in-europe-the-echr-and-beyond -video-speech-by-dunj/16809ebe73).

1.4 The values of democracy, human rights and international law

To demonstrate clearly what the European Union and its members – including Germany – have unequivocally committed themselves to, I will briefly document the basic principles below.

Article 1 of the German Basic Law (the constitution of the Federal Republic of Germany) begins with the words:

> (1) Human dignity shall be inviolable. To respect and protect it shall be the duty of all state authority.

> (2) The German people therefore acknowledge inviolable and inalienable human rights as the basis of every community, of peace and of justice in the world.

These two clauses bind the German government to human rights. Similar commitments to human rights and human dignity are also found in the constitutions of other European states and in the Lisbon Treaty, the basis of the European Union, in which Article 1(a) states:

> The Union is founded on the values of respect for human dignity, freedom, democracy, equality, the rule of law and respect for human rights, including the rights of persons belonging to minorities. These values are common to the Member States in a society in which pluralism, non-discrimination, tolerance, justice, solidarity and equality between women and men prevail.

It is true, of course, that these basic formulations convey no justiciable rights. They do, however, prohibit asylum and refugee policy from simply abandoning human rights, as if these rights were relevant only to domestic policy and as if the European Union or the individual states could insulate their asylum and refugee policy from them. Below are the core formulations of our human rights obligations.

The 1948 United Nations Universal Declaration of Human Rights

The United Nations Universal Declaration of Human Rights is often quoted, yet its impact on respect for human rights in refugee policy leaves much to be desired. It may therefore be helpful to reflect on the intentions and motivations of its initiators, in the wake of World War II, and its wording in relation to refugee and asylum policy. They are expressed in the preamble and in the first and fourteenth articles. The preamble begins:

Whereas recognition of the inherent dignity and of the equal and inalienable rights of all members of the human family is the foundation of freedom, justice and peace in the world,

Whereas disregard and contempt for human rights have resulted in barbarous acts which have outraged the conscience of mankind, and the advent of a world in which human beings shall enjoy freedom of speech and belief and freedom from fear and want has been proclaimed as the highest aspiration of the common people,

Whereas it is essential, if man is not to be compelled to have recourse, as a last resort, to rebellion against tyranny and oppression, that human rights should be protected by the rule of law,

Whereas it is essential to promote the development of friendly relations between nations,

Whereas the peoples of the United Nations have in the Charter reaffirmed their faith in fundamental human rights, in the dignity and worth of the human person and in the equal rights of men and women and have determined to promote social progress and better standards of life in larger freedom,

Whereas Member States have pledged themselves to achieve, in co-operation with the United Nations, the promotion of universal respect for and observance of human rights and fundamental freedoms,

Whereas a common understanding of these rights and freedoms is of the greatest importance for the full realization of this pledge,

Now, therefore,

The General Assembly,

Proclaims this Universal Declaration of Human Rights as the common standard of achievement for all peoples and all nations, to the end that every individual and every organ of society, keeping this Declaration constantly in mind, shall strive by teaching and education to promote respect for these rights and freedoms and by progressive measures, national and international, to secure their universal and effective recognition and observance, both among the peoples of Member States themselves and among the peoples of territories under their jurisdiction.

The first article states:

All human beings are born free and equal in dignity and rights. They are endowed with reason and conscience and should act towards one another in a spirit of brotherhood.

On asylum and refugee policy, the pertinent article of the Universal Declaration of Human Rights (Article 14) states:

1. Everyone has the right to seek and to enjoy in other countries asylum from persecution.

2. This right may not be invoked in the case of prosecutions genuinely arising from non-political crimes or from acts contrary to the purposes and principles of the United Nations.

While the declaration is not binding under international law, states are officially committed to it if they explicitly make reference to the declaration in their constitutions.

The Geneva Refugee Convention of 1951 and the extended 1967 Protocol

The Geneva Refugee Convention (originally titled "The Convention Relating to the Status of Refugees") is the basis of asylum and refugee law under international law and thus the guideline for the EU's political actions. It came into being as a reaction to the numerous population displacements of the 20th century. In particular, the experience of the Nazi policy of persecution and extermination and the ensuing population displacements made protection against political and governmental persecution a key issue. The Geneva Convention on Refugees initially applied only to those claiming asylum in Europe. According to the convention, a refugee is a person who,

as a result of events occurring before 1 January 1951 and owing to well-founded fear of being persecuted for reasons of race, religion, nationality, membership of a particular social group or political opinion, is outside the country of his nationality and is unable or, owing to such fear, is unwilling to avail himself of the protection of that country [...] (Article 1(2))

This narrow temporal and geographical limitation was lifted in the extended 1967 Protocol, which significantly expanded the concept of protection to address the changed realities of the refugee situation. To date, some 169 states have acceded to the convention and/or the Protocol. This 1967 extension is also pertinent to current circumstances – for instance, the need to take into account new causes of displacement such as the climate crisis – and it demonstrates that a further extension is possible and, indeed, may be necessary.

The core of the Geneva Refugee Convention and the additional Protocol is the principle of non-refoulement set out in Article 33. It prohibits the expulsion or return of refugees (that is, their refoulement) to areas where their life or freedom would be threatened because of their "race, religion, nationality, membership of a particular social group or political opinion". The principle of non-refoulement cannot be invoked by a person if there are justified grounds for believing

> that he or she has committed a crime against peace, a war crime or a crime against humanity as defined in international treaties [...] that he or she has committed a serious non-political crime outside the host country before being admitted as a refugee there; that he or she has been guilty of acts contrary to the purposes and principles of the United Nations. (Article 1(F))

Other international human rights conventions, such as the UN Convention against Torture, also include the principle of non-refoulement, and as a result the principle is now regarded as customary international law. This requirement therefore provides protection, though in practice this can be implemented in varying ways. In the European Union individuals can be recognised as refugees on the basis of individual political persecution or or be granted subsidiary or temporary protection if they are fleeing from a civil war.

The following considerations do not aim to offer a comparative legal assessment of asylum and refugee policy but rather aim to provide a political response to displacement and migration situations, which must be distinguished from each other but which may be determined by overlapping or similar situations. Politicians may act only within the law, but if there were the political will to overcome the current state of affairs – which is in contravention of human rights – this would not only be in line with the spirit of human rights, but also, as political experience makes clear, be perfectly feasible from a legal standpoint.

It is plain that EU asylum and refugee policy as currently practised contradicts both human rights and the obligations imposed by international law – for example, in its violation of the principle of non-refoulement. As a result of European decisions, many asylum seekers are currently living on EU soil or at its external borders under conditions that contravene human dignity and the rights set out in the Geneva Refugee Convention.

The European Convention on Human Rights and the EU Charter of Fundamental Rights

The European Convention on Human Rights (or "The Convention for the Protection of Human Rights and Fundamental Freedoms") and the EU Charter of Fundamental Rights are also binding on the European Union's asylum and refugee policy.

The convention, which is continually being developed by means of additional protocols, was adopted by the Council of Europe in 1950 and it entered into force in 1953. The EU has not yet acceded to the convention by means of a treaty, although it is obliged to do so by Article 6 of the Treaty on European Union. Nonetheless, it has been ratified by all the member states, which in turn binds the EU. This means that the judgments of the European Court of Human Rights, which monitors compliance with the convention and can be appealed to by all citizens, are also binding on the EU. It must be said, however, that there are no provisions for the imposition of sanctions in the case of violations. In response to the court's ruling against the return of refugees to Libya (in the Hirsi Jamaa case), the EU reacted to public pressure, as described above, but at the same time it tried to introduce functional alternatives – which would, it hoped, evade censure – to the actions deemed to contravene human rights. The EU is thus, in practice, pursuing a policy of contravening the spirit of the European Convention on Human Rights.

The articles of the convention implicitly contain references to displacement, asylum and migration.[11] The convention may therefore be considered a normative and value-oriented reference basis in this respect.

Although the EU Charter of Fundamental Rights was adopted in 2000, it did not come into effect until December 2009, nine years later. It was originally intended to form part of the European Constitution and thus hold a prominent status for all European citizens. Unfortunately, this prominence was much reduced following the failure in France and the Netherlands of referendums to approve the European Constitution. The

---

11   "Under the ECHR, it is acknowledged that the prohibition of inhuman and degrading treatment under Article 3 includes refoulement to such conditions" (Schmalz, D. (2019) "Zur Reichweite von Menschenrechtspflichten: Zugang zu Schutz an den Grenzen Europas", *Newsletter Menschenrechte,* (5): 367–376). The European Court of Human Rights referenced Article 3 of the convention when they established the illegality of refoulement in the Hirsi case in 2009. An attempt is also being made to derive a positive obligation to protect on the basis of Article 2 (the right to life). Furthermore, Article 4 of the Fourth Protocol to the Convention explicitly prohibits collective expulsion.

charter became binding when it was incorporated into the Lisbon Treaty in December 2009.

Its purpose and sources are succinctly summarised in its preamble:

> This Charter reaffirms, with due regard for the powers and tasks of the Community and the Union and the principle of subsidiarity, the rights as they result, in particular, from the constitutional traditions and international obligations common to the Member States, the Treaty on European Union, the Community Treaties, the European Convention for the Protection of Human Rights and Fundamental Freedoms, the Social Charters adopted by the Community and by the Council of Europe and the case-law of the Court of Justice of the European Communities and of the European Court of Human Rights.

Refugee and asylum policy are covered by Articles 18 and 19. Article 18:

> The right to asylum shall be guaranteed with due respect for the rules of the Geneva Convention of 28 July 1951 and the Protocol of 31 January 1967 relating to the status of refugees and in accordance with the Treaty establishing the European Community.

Article 19:

> Protection in the event of removal, expulsion or extradition

> 1. Collective expulsions are prohibited.

> 2. No one may be removed, expelled or extradited to a State where there is a serious risk that he or she would be subjected to the death penalty, torture or other inhuman or degrading treatment or punishment.

The EU thus reaffirmed its commitment to the Geneva Refugee Convention in the form of the Charter of Fundamental Rights. Does its elaboration in the European Union's asylum law do justice to this commitment?

Right of asylum in the European Union

The creation of common European asylum procedures has been a declared goal of the European Union for some 20 years. The high point of the EU's attempts to organise a humane refugee and asylum policy was in 1999 in Tampere, Finland, where, in view of the right to asylum, a decision was taken to set up a "Common European Asylum System" that would strictly adhere to the Geneva Refugee Convention and, in particular, to the requirement under international law of avoiding refoulement from a European country to a situation where an individual's life might be in danger. It is on the basis of this requirement that Article 78 of the Treaty on the Functioning of the European Union – the EU's core treaty – states that every third-country national in need of international protection shall be offered an appropriate status and that compliance with the principle of non-refoulement shall be ensured.[12]

Despite this, attempts to establish a truly common European asylum procedure that in practice meets the legal standards have been unsuccessful. Two particular shortcomings need to be highlighted: there are considerable deficiencies, firstly, in access to the asylum procedure and, secondly, in the division of responsibility between member states for arriving asylum seekers (the previously described absence of a "distribution" system). Both problems are intertwined, as the member states that are separated from the EU's external borders have attempted, through the Dublin III Regulation, to make the border states primarily responsible for asylum procedures without establishing a binding procedure for sharing that responsibility. Moreover, the regulations (the directly applicable legislation) cover only responsibility for asylum procedures and registration of asylum seekers. The important aspects of reception, procedural steps and the question of who qualifies as eligible for protection are laid down only in directives, which first need to be transposed into national law to become applicable, and whose implementation is the responsibility of member states.

EU asylum law thus consists, in essence, of two regulations and several associated directives. The two regulations are the aforementioned Dublin III Regulation, which regulates the responsibility of the member states for asylum procedures, and the Eurodac Regulation, which regulates the registration of asylum seekers. The 1990 Dublin Convention was replaced by the Dublin II Regulation in 2003, and all EU member states have been subject to the Dublin III Regulation since 2014. It is a key component of the desired Common European Asylum System and stipulates that the

---

12   In addition, the treaty also specifies in paragraph 3 of the same article that, in the event of an emergency situation in one or more member states caused by a sudden influx of third-country nationals, the Council, acting on a proposal from the Commission, may adopt provisional measures in favour of the member states concerned, after seeking the opinion of the European Parliament. This resulted in the unsuccessful attempt to introduce a compulsory relocation quota, as previously explained.

state where asylum seekers first set foot on EU soil is the one responsible for examining their asylum applications. This is to ensure that at least one state declares itself responsible for the assessment procedures, and it also aims to prevent asylum seekers from simultaneously applying for protection in several countries.

Though explicitly regulating the responsibility of the member states was intended to ensure access to and responsibility for the procedures, its design was flawed from the outset due to the imbalance between the countries of first entry at the external borders and the member states without an external border. Exceptions to this first-country-of-entry rule are made, however, if asylum seekers have family or close relatives in another country. In such cases, they are permitted to move to that country under the framework of family reunification. In addition, other EU member states may at any time voluntarily accept responsibility for the asylum procedure via the so-called sovereignty clause set out in Article 17 of the Dublin III Regulation. This can be done either for humanitarian reasons at the request of another member state under paragraph 2, or, under paragraph 1, without the need to link the reception to specific conditions.[13]

In principle, however, the primary responsibility falls to the first country of entry. Asylum seekers are therefore obliged to remain in that country while their application for asylum is processed. If they travel independently to another EU member state, the destination country must deport the asylum seekers to the country of first entry within a very limited timeframe (six months) or the responsibility for the asylum procedure is transferred to the destination country.[14] These "secondary movements" are a particular thorn in the side of landlocked countries, as they are obliged to expend considerable effort to quickly determine whether they are responsible and, if not, to rapidly return the asylum seekers to the country of first entry.

The Eurodac Regulation is intended to prevent asylum seekers from independently travelling on to another EU member state by registering

---

13   In a legal opinion from the Friedrich Ebert Stiftung on the question of direct EU funding for municipalities that wish to take in refugees voluntarily, Dr Sina Fontana concludes that Article 17(1) of the Dublin III Regulation is "a discretionary provision that may be construed as an obligation to accept". (Fontana, S. (2021) "Integrations- & Entwicklungsfonds: Rechtsgutachten zur Umsetzbarkeit einer EU-geförderten kommunalen Integrations- und Entwicklungsinitiative". Friedrich Ebert Stiftung, p. 5 (https://library.fes.de/pdf-files/bueros/bruessel/17884.pdf).)

14   See Article 13 of Regulation (EU) 604/2013 (the Dublin III Regulation). If a person remains in a member state for at least five months without interruption, the responsibility for the procedure is transferred to that member state.

each asylum seeker upon arrival in the country of first entry. Backed up by a fingerprinting system, the Eurodac Regulation is thus intended to ensure the implementation of the Dublin Regulation, that is, to ensure the responsibility of the member states for asylum procedures.

The actual asylum procedures will, however, continue to be carried out by the member states. Three directives are intended to guarantee common standards within the European Union. The Qualification Directive defines who is entitled to protection, the Reception Directive deals with the manner in which the reception and treatment of asylum seekers is organised, and the Asylum Procedures Directive sets out the basic principles of asylum procedures. Despite these common directives, the asylum procedures of the respective member states differ considerably. This is true not only for the question of who is considered eligible for protection, which is regulated by the Qualification Directive, but also for access to procedures, procedural guarantees, and accommodation and care.[15] These are the legislative aspects.

A report commissioned by the European Parliament in 2020 on the implementation of the Dublin III Regulation also reveals that the treatment and reception meted out to those who reach Europe in no way accords with what was actually envisaged for the Common European Asylum System.[16] The report details how practice often falls short of the required regulations, to the detriment of asylum seekers (through failings such as poor access to legal aid and information or criminalisation of nongovernmental organisations (NGOs) that wish to fill this gap). It also shows that the "hotspots" in Greece and Italy totally fail to meet the European Commission's objectives, on the basis of which they were established. These findings underline the inadequacy of the documentation on asylum procedures, the irrationality and expense of returning refugees to their countries of first entry, and the high degree of insecurity and high costs that secondary movements impose on asylum seekers.

Why is the EU failing so dramatically and shamefully in its asylum and refugee policy? What binds its members together that would allow a common policy across national frontiers?

---

15   Bast, J., F. von Harbou and J. Wessels (2020) *Human Rights Challenges to European Migration Policy: The REMAP Study* (Baden-Baden: Nomos).

16   Scherrer, A. (2020) "Dublin Regulation on international protection application: European Implementation Assessment". European Parliamentary Research Service (www.europarl.europa.eu/RegData/etudes/STUD/2020/642813/EPRS_STU(2020) 642813_EN.pdf).

1.5 The primacy of nation states and their tactical interests

The European Union was founded by the European nation states. Its supreme decision-making body, and the decisive political body when it comes to refugee policy, is the European Council, which brings together the heads of national governments. Intergovernmental negotiation also takes place in the Council of Ministers, between the ministers of the national governments – including the interior ministers, who are responsible for refugee policy.

The national governments are put in power through national elections. In election campaigns they run on issues that they think their national voters will support. Conversely, candidates and the parties that nominate them are usually reluctant to raise issues that may encounter opposition, even if only briefly. A classic example of this avoidance strategy is the cautiousness around the desire to raise taxes. Parties avoid the issue because they always expect to be punished by the voters.

This applies to an even greater degree to a truly European refugee policy. National governments fear the political requirement of accepting and supporting refugees in accordance with the human rights and legal obligations to which they and the European Union have committed themselves and that are documented above, because they believe it would lose them too many votes. In particular, this is because radical right-wing parties are inciting anti-refugee sentiment in almost all European countries (with rare exceptions, such as Portugal).

The problem extends beyond the refugee issue: these opportunist considerations and motives prevent and impede solidarity among European states, leading many problems to remain unsolved. They also explain why the EU is extremely slow in tackling new issues. The decision to embark on an unprecedented innovation in community financing following the pandemic – the recovery fund – was, as previously discussed, an exception.

However, this recent exception also highlights that, even in the European Council, powerful members such as Germany and determined politicians could have adopted a different policy that would have positively affected the overall development of refugee policy. The "fear" that was induced by the refugee influx in 2015 and that subsequently prevented the establishment of a humane refugee policy in its aftermath was not the result of keeping the borders open. Rather, it was caused by the subsequent outrage whipped up in particular by Bavaria's Christian Social Union, the sister party of Germany's Christian Democratic Union.

One thing is thus clear: it is not the EU's institutional structure and certainly not the original European institutions such as the European Parliament and the European Commission that stand in the way of a solidarity-based, future-oriented policy. The main reason that such a policy is lacking is the politics of the nation states, whose governments are short-sightedly focused on maintaining power at the national level. This includes the German government, which, due to its considerable power, bears a particular responsibility and could have opted to act in a very different, strategic manner. Not only has Europe failed, it is above all the nation states in the EU, not least Germany, that have failed.

This is, of course, true of European governments beyond Germany and the Visegrád states of Poland, Czechia, Slovakia and Hungary. There was, furthermore, an absence of genuinely proactive initiatives from the Commission, which, then as now, was also lacking in imagination. For example, it could have done more to involve and support the EU's Committee of the Regions and the municipalities in this respect, but it chose instead to avoid tension with the national governments from the outset.

How Europe acts depends in large part on the political colour of its national governments. It is clear that the more conservative those governments are, the less solidarity they show towards neighbouring states and the more hostile they are towards asylum seekers. Even social democratic parties are not immune to this populist hostility, as the example of Denmark's social democratic government shows.

It is only the European Parliament that has repeatedly made attempts to put forward a more humane asylum and refugee policy, but even there, the political majorities have impeded a genuine breakthrough. There is also, of course, the problem that the European Parliament is unable to prevail against the European Council.

The fact that both the EU and the German government are well aware of the contradiction between their proclaimed values and their actual politics can be seen in the camouflaging clichés they use to conceal their inhumane policy of isolationism and deterrence. They defend their objective of closing the external borders and monitoring them more closely – and, as far as possible, of leaving no gaps through which refugees can set foot on European soil – by saying that they want to "end the people-smuggling trade" and "protect the refugees from undertaking the dangerous Mediterranean crossing". The language used makes it sound as if they were motivated by their great concern for the refugees. In reality they could protect them more effectively by opening up more legal routes to

Europe and, for example, by increasing the resettlement rate. In addition, they could design and put in place a coherent, well-thought-out asylum and refugee policy, which would include provisions for work permits and immigration and also integrate embedded development cooperation. A humane refugee policy is only possible within such a broad context. This is a topic I will return to.

What is it, besides moral anguish, that drives us to urgently flag up the dangers of this contradiction and promote the alternative of a humane European refugee policy?

The dangerous consequences of moral inconsistency

To sum things up in a single sentence, we Europeans are harming ourselves due to this moral contradiction. We are destroying our cohesion and the basis of our democracies. We are squandering the opportunities for a rich, constructive and meaningful common future, both within Europe and in the global North–South relationship.

The cultural basis of people living together in democratic freedom is trust in their fellow human beings and the reliability of democratic institutions, political procedures and promises. Maintaining this trust requires the transparency and supervision of those institutions in order to ensure their survival. Trust between people and within democratic institutions is never total, but its complete disappearance in our societies would destroy social harmony and leave only violence as a means for citizens to assert themselves. Having lost their belief in the effectiveness of justice, citizens would then act only in accordance with their particularist interests. The more perceptive members of society take refuge in cynicism when confronted by moral contradictions. They begin to show contempt for values they are unable to fulfil or quote them only with derision. "I don't recall people in the European Commission giving much thought to values," as a long-time employee of the institution said.

Democratic societies generally accept that promises and statements politicians make about their own behaviour need to be taken with a pinch of salt. But when it comes to European refugee policy, the moral self-contradiction in their approach and in almost every other aspect is glaringly apparent. It is an undeniable, unavoidable fact. When the topic is discussed, the response from those defending the current European refugee policy is generally not, "We're acting in accordance with our values," but rather, "If we adhered to our values, millions of refugees would come to Europe. We wouldn't be able to cope with that." Self-contradiction is

---

therefore supposedly inevitable. I will return to this claim, which we can file under the "pull factor", later.

It is clear, however, that not only are the repeatedly proclaimed values meaningless in practice but their disregard also jeopardises our self-esteem. It really would not be possible to be more self-contradictory! The question is why this blatant moral self-contradiction is so dangerous and undermining to democracy and Europe.

If this gap between values and practice were truly inevitable, then the European Union would not stand a chance. That said, I would like to show that it is something we can avoid and that a humane refugee policy is possible.

The case could be argued that it is possible to respect human rights within the EU and Germany while ignoring them only externally, such as when it comes to refugees and our neighbours – in Africa, for example. This argument is implicit in the often-heard claim that we need to close the external frontiers in order to keep the internal European borders open in accordance with the Schengen Agreement. The moral cost of such a radical exclusion of the external world, which cannot be achieved without contradicting our values, would in this view either have no impact on our internal relationships or perhaps even benefit them. This could be true if we stopped invoking the very values that supposedly determine our actions, but that would mean that these values would also lose their validity in Europe's internal relationships.

We therefore cannot deny our values, as doing so would deprive the European Union of the very basis of its legitimacy, something that even the most hardened cynics would not dare to do. On the contrary, we continue with our duplicity and deceit. But why should our fellow citizens and political opponents in the EU or Germany believe that governments will act in a trustworthy manner and keep their promises within Europe when they obviously do not do so to partners outside it?

In other words, you cannot slice and dice credibility as it suits you and choose when to act in accordance with it. If that were the case, I would always have to ask myself whether my counterpart in a conversation was switching into hypocritical mode – in effect, whether they were lying to me. No one would be able to tell when another considered the time right for dishonesty. Here we have to make a decision: either we act credibly, or we do not.

It is this logic and the absence of those definitive decisions that have led to the notable decline in trust that we have long been able to observe both within our national democracies and throughout Europe. This is what the many years of hypocrisy – between citizens and between nation states – have given rise to. It began before the start of the refugee crisis and is also taking place outside Europe. The crisis of trust in the EU is growing at the same pace as the solidarity between governments is diminishing. This loss of trust has now grown sharply, yet the EU is still with us. The solidarity shown in the decision to set up the post-pandemic recovery fund has even given rise to fresh trust and helped stabilise the EU. Does that mean we can simply maintain the self-contradiction? No, because the level of mistrust remains high and continues to erode credibility.

We can see this when we ask ourselves why the EU as a whole has in recent years increasingly lost its ability to act, not only on the refugee question but, even more visibly, in international and global economic and trade policy. Moral self-contradiction prevents Europe, as a global player, from agreeing on fundamental objectives and procedures that would enable it to exert its influence in a convincing and effective manner. Where is our common position towards Russia? Or China? Both powers (and in particular China), whose governments despise our democracies and our emphasis on human rights, are direct competitors. They are taking advantage of intra-European mistrust, in particular in Greece and the Balkans, but also in Hungary and Bulgaria, in order to forge new alliances with the disillusioned countries and weaken the European Union by intensifying internal mistrust.

If we insist on democratic politics and the democratic way of life, but betray these same values by our own actions at the very moment when other countries demand solidarity from us – as happened with Greece in 2015 – we will, as a result, lose the very political influence and authority in the world with which we seek to protect our way of life. Some may consider a quality such as authority too soft an instrument to protect a liberal and socially secure lifestyle. What help is it against a military attack such as that of the Russians against Ukraine? In fact the present lack of support for the public defence of Ukraine by a number of African countries is also due to the growing hypocrisy of the EU concerning human rights in its closing the borders brutally against refugees from Africa.

In Southern and South-Eastern Europe too, significant gaps have recently become apparent in the authority and credibility of the EU's solidarity – in the supply of Covid vaccines, for example. Both China and Russia were happy to draw the loyalty of the South-Eastern European states away from Brussels by supplying vaccines. It no longer goes without saying that the European Union is attractive to the societies of South-Eastern Europe.

If we are to build a world worth living in, credibility is the most durable power we possess. Military power lets us deter, instil fear or destroy, and – with luck and good planning – police civil reconstruction. That would then be a first step towards constructive power, which, as Hannah Arendt has stated, lies in the ability to motivate and engage natural allies to undertake joint projects, such as peace and development. A humane refugee policy is therefore also in the interests of Europeans themselves, if we take a long-term view. But they will only be able to act together when they overcome self-contradiction.

2 | What are the possible alternatives to the current European refugee policy?

2.1 The key political challenge: regulating the reliable decentralised reception of refugees in Europe

If national governments, which have so far de facto determined the EU asylum and refugee policy, are unable to agree on a common policy of solidarity, and if we do not want to allow the inhumanity that happens on a daily basis – and the concomitant destructive moral self-contradiction – to continue, then we must look for alternatives. And they do exist!

The key challenge from the perspective of the people arriving as refugees and migrants is gaining access to protection in the European Union through legal and secure ways. From the perspective of the European Union and its member states, on the other hand, the key challenge is the fair division of responsibility for the implementation of asylum procedures and for accommodating and caring for refugees, which means agreeing on a reliable distribution mechanism. Yet this approach is inhumane, and misleading from a strategic perspective. It implies that it is a matter of sharing a burden, not a process in which all parties attempt to adopt a procedure that is as consensual and fair as possible, and to the benefit of all.

That is why I use the term "decentralised reception" rather than "distribution". This must be regulated in a responsible manner, while ensuring that access to the asylum process is not linked to an existing offer of reception. A reliable decentralised reception system is necessary to avoid the prison-like and overcrowded initial reception centres with inhumane living conditions. It would also address the understandable concerns of the first-arrival states in the south and east of the EU (Bulgaria, Greece, Malta, Italy and Spain) about being overwhelmed both socially and in terms of infrastructure if they alone are made to bear the responsibility of organising and financing arrival and asylum procedures. In addition, these states have no certainty on the next steps for those entitled to protection in Europe or those currently without a defined claim to protection. These concerns reveal the fundamental conflict between the EU's external border states and those without an external border – a conflict that has existed ever since asylum and migration policy was communitised. The EU's external border states have no interest in registering new arrivals, as this would in effect make them responsible for the majority of all procedures, while the inland states want them to carry out the registrations in order to impede asylum seekers from independently continuing to other member states ("secondary movement"). I discussed the dysfunctionality of the Dublin Regulation in the previous chapter.

However, decentralised reception can function reliably only if it is agreed on voluntarily, as it is impossible to enforce reliability in the reception of refugees. There have been numerous attempts to draw up a "distribution" regulation that is binding on every country, but these have not succeeded. The European Commission's most recent proposal, in September 2020, also effectively failed. The reasons are by now familiar and always the same. The proposal should have been negotiated and adopted by the end of 2020, but no conclusion is in sight. That means that there is no imminent prospect of all the EU member states acting together and being obliged to admit their share of refugees. Any such obligation will not work, and those politicians who remain wedded to this provision are, in reality, helping to ensure that nothing changes and perhaps even wishing to prevent a humane response to the refugee question.

The prevailing legal interpretation in Germany, and in other EU states, stresses that the power to decide on the reception of refugees lies with national governments alone. For good reasons, this is now being called into question, but since we want to see a humane refugee policy implemented as quickly as possible, it is pragmatic to work on the basis of prevailing opinion, which means that we cannot bypass national governments. Given the decision-making powers of the member states' national politicians in the European Council, have we reached an impasse?

To escape the stalemate in asylum and refugee policy, it is necessary to negotiate a voluntary agreement, combined with positive incentives to receive refugees, including financial incentives. This will help replace the basic paradigm of "commitment" – which considers the reception of refugees to be a burden – with a positive one, in which reception can be perceived as beneficial and a win-win situation for all.

2.2 Voluntary participation and positive incentives instead of sanctions: enhanced competences of municipalities

This win-win situation will be achieved when reception is organised in such a way that ethical values, human rights and the rule of law are reconciled with the interests of the citizens, who, as a result, do not perceive the observance of values as a sacrifice of their own interests.

In principle, this is also possible at the national level, if admitting refugees is combined with a shrewd immigration policy. I will come back to this connection later. There is, however, a major obstacle to this approach. The nation states continue to be very inflexible, in part due to the previously outlined politicisation of the issue through the rise of numerous right-wing and populist parties in Europe, which sometimes drive competing parties to adopt aspects of their own policies or which – as in Hungary and Poland – manage to gain power themselves. The level at which interests (long-term ones in particular) and values can be combined most easily, most transparently and with citizens' consent is the municipality. At this level, a successful refugee policy can be combined with a successful extension of effective civic engagement, something that is compatible with representative democracy.

*

Close to 80% of Europeans now live in cities and municipalities. These are where people live their lives, where the most energy is consumed and where decisive measures must be undertaken to stop climate change, conserve resources and renew and improve infrastructure, particularly with regard to mobility. They are the places where citizens seek a sense of community in sports or cultural initiatives and associations, in addition to being an important focus for digital development. At the same time, the consequences of demographic change are often felt most severely in cities and municipalities. Across Europe, smaller towns and communities – often those with historically rich traditions, culture and especially architecture – are being abandoned. Beautiful old towns are in danger of falling into ruin, particularly in Spain and Italy. This experience must be creatively combined with the imperative of – and benefits from – increased commitment to democratic participation and sustainability, including a humane refugee policy.

In line with the 17 Sustainable Development Goals adopted by the United Nations in 2015, planning for a sustainable future is becoming increasingly important and requires the support of the citizenry, particularly in cities and municipalities. New technologies and increasingly diverse societies are leading to changes in needs and lifestyles with each new generation. They bring with them the possibility of working from anywhere, which can make it easier for parents to reconcile their working and family lives. Communication is also increasingly streamlined, facilitating greater citizen participation in municipal planning.

Goal 11 of the Sustainable Development Goals advocates sustainable cities, with sustainability referring not only to climate protection and energy saving but also to the shaping of interpersonal social relationships. Goal 17 recommends partnership as a structural principle for policymaking, both locally and at a global level. Development is of importance not only to the so-called developing countries but to everyone. The Global North needs to develop too, preferably in partnership with the South.

This fits together very well with a refugee and migration policy that tackles the complex political realities and recognises that there are always particular reasons for displacement and migration while acknowledging that both have occurred repeatedly in the past and will probably continue to do so long into the future. The more we can organise the response to these displacements collaboratively – in the interest of the common good and with due respect for the enormous diversity of interests – the better the outcomes for all. That is why the structuring of asylum, refugee and migration policies is of key importance to our future and can determine whether we work together in peace, freedom and sustainable prosperity in a relationship based on solidarity, or continue to destroy ourselves in bloody conflicts.

It is in cities and municipalities that refugees arrive and settle. They must therefore ensure that refugees encounter a good reception, in terms of housing, work, education, health and all other cultural requirements that will enable them to create a new life for themselves, to feel at ease in their new country and to participate constructively in the life of the community.

More than 500 cities and municipalities in the EU have now agreed to receive more refugees, even in the absence of the incentive system I have proposed.[1]

---

1   "Europe welcomes", Greens/EFA in the European Parliament (www.europewelcomes. org); "Moving cities", Robert Bosch Foundation (www.bosch-stiftung.de/en/project/mov ing-cities).

2.3 Reception of refugees by municipal development councils for sustainable integration into the host society

As a first step, I therefore propose that far greater consideration should be given to cities and municipalities as actors in a humane European refugee policy. They can be the starting point for the political initiative to receive refugees voluntarily, in their own interest as well as that of the refugees.

To prepare and organise this efficiently and sustainably, I would suggest setting up development advisory boards in municipalities. These will advise on the long-term development plan of the municipality and prepare for its implementation. These boards would be the place to consider the demographic development of the community, as well as the new training needs and new economic opportunities that would result from a changing labour force. They would advise on how municipal infrastructures should expand to adapt to those economic changes, and also to provide sports, education and further training, to increase the available housing, and to offer opportunities for cultural development and the social integration of all those living in the municipality. In a pluralist democratic society, integration is fundamentally an ongoing challenge and task for society as a whole, not only in connection with migration, but also, for example, because of the ever-widening gulf between rich and poor.

Mayors could help give this long-term planning a solid foundation by holding meetings at regular intervals (perhaps four times a year) to discuss the community's future on the basis of the assessment of the administration and other models of expertise. These meetings could bring together representatives from the elected municipal council and their administration as well as unelected representatives of NGOs, citizens' initiatives and companies.

Such meetings must be well prepared and professionally moderated if they are not to end in frustration. Further training must be offered and financed to enable moderation by well-known local personalities (preferably heads of sports clubs, schools, and so on, rather than the mayors or chief executives of the local administration). If this is not done, communities will understandably resist taking on new tasks and forming new institutions at a time when many of them are in financially precarious circumstances. Democracy cannot be achieved without funding.

Municipal administrations often oppose any involvement by citizens' initiatives and companies when preparing their municipal development plans, which is why it is important to explain the benefits of early inclusion. The way things traditionally work is that the administration draws up plans and then, if necessary, presents them to the public. This often leads to conflicts in the administration, which may feel that its efforts are not respected, and among citizens, who feel that they have not been sufficiently consulted or involved in the planning. It also leads to delays in implementing the plans and to frustration among citizens, because the public presentation of the plans gives citizens little opportunity to influence them. As a result, citizens then feel that their participation is a sham.

The alternative procedure outlined here does not prevent elected officials from making the final decision, which is a necessity in a representative democracy. Nonetheless, engaging in cooperation from the outset instils a desire in those elected representatives to implement what has been elaborated over a considerable period of time.

Expanding democratic participation is more comprehensive and much more straightforward and feasible than the "citizens' councils" that Wolfgang Schäuble promoted while he was president of the Bundestag. Firstly, municipal development advisory boards deal with not just one or two topics but the entire range of topics and interests that concern a municipality. That means that their focus is not solely on one topic or interest to the exclusion of all others. The real art of politics is, after all, that of weighing up competing interests. Secondly, such a solution generally offers many more citizens the opportunity to engage politically over the long term and in line with their real-life interests, rather than merely in the form of temporary "further education", as in the case of limited-topic citizens' councils, which are generally restricted to around 160 participants. Thirdly and finally, having clarified the perspective of practical implementation, the further training and political experience gained in this process by local citizens will also represent a sustainable investment in the community and in its political empowerment. Citizens' councils, on the other hand, are dissolved following their intensive "training" meetings, rather like an extended weekend visit to a political academy. This is not sustainable.

*

If, under this proposal, municipalities reach the conclusion that they would like to receive refugees in order to ensure their municipal development and the maintenance of their public services (particularly important factors for such conclusions are demographics and the available workforce, including its training and further education), they can submit a formal offer to receive them. The football clubs in rural Saxony-Anhalt, for example, are committed to this goal in order to ensure a flow of young players to their junior clubs, which is necessary due to constant migration away from these areas.

There is often a worry that this procedure could lead to "cherry-picking" and that only very "useful" refugees would be invited by municipalities. Committed NGOs would therefore need to play their part in the development advisory boards, as good politics depends on citizens' involvement. Nonetheless, there is sufficient common sense in municipalities and among companies based in them to reject any such instrumentalisation. It would, of course, also be possible to draw up regulations linked to financing conditions. We should not, however, underestimate the civic spirit of our society!

To ensure that sensible decisions are taken with as wide-ranging and long-term a perspective as possible, it is also important to include the expertise of the refugees themselves and of migration associations, the results of research into migration, and, in particular, advice from expert sources with an interest in the development of the community, such as local universities.

When a broad-based approach is taken for planning for the future, with the administration and elected representatives addressing the future together with local citizens and companies, there is, as I have said, a very high probability that the decisions made will also be implemented. Looking at it from the opposite perspective, this procedure avoids a situation in which the administration comes up with what it considers to be good ideas and is frustrated when the public presentation of the resulting plan meets with rejection and objections from citizens who respond unfavourably because they were not consulted. Demographic changes will ensure that we have even more citizens who can volunteer and get involved.

The outcome of the planning consultations should of course be made public (for example, by publishing it on the municipality's home page) and discussed in the district. In the age of digitalisation, this should be a matter of course. All age groups must be ensured access. In connection with our topic of a humane refugee policy, the home page would also give information about the municipality's offer to receive refugees. This would be the first step towards a "matching system" that would coordinate the needs of local communities with those of refugees. This is already under consideration, and preparatory work is currently being undertaken in this regard. Malisa Zobel and I have put forward some key points for such a matching system below.

2.4 A matching system that reconciles the interests and needs of refugees and municipalities

As previously explained in Chapter 1.3, asylum seekers have so far had little say over which EU member state they are allowed to settle in, let alone which municipality, since the Dublin III Regulation puts the responsibility for the majority of all asylum procedures on the member states with an external Schengen border.

The fundamental notion of a matching mechanism is to make use of the diversity of municipalities and populations in a targeted way in order to ensure a "fit" between asylum seekers and host municipalities, rather than to randomly distribute asylum seekers among member states and municipalities in a top-down approach. The challenge here is to find good matches for all the parties involved (in other words, not only for the most qualified asylum seekers and the most attractive communities). To achieve these matches, municipalities and asylum seekers need to be involved at an early stage in the process so that they can ensure their interests, needs and offers are taken into account. If possible, each asylum seeker should receive a list with more than one suitable municipality at the end of the matching process and then be able to choose between the offers.

Such a novel system does, of course, need to take a number of challenges into consideration. These challenges are political and normative as well as technical. In political terms, it is a question of assembling a majority within the member states for a "distribution" mechanism. Normative criteria must be developed and applied to ensure that the absolute number of asylum seekers to be relocated is not reduced. In other words, the proposed approach should result in more and not fewer asylum seekers finding a place of residence in another EU member state than at present. The new system should also ensure that municipalities do not "cherry-pick" among refugees. As for the technical feasibility of such a system, a number of respected researchers have worked on devising a methodological basis for such matching mechanisms. Advances in evaluating large amounts of data by more powerful computers and by algorithmic analytical methods allow comparisons to be made between the preferences of a large number of participating actors. The following provides an outline of the political challenges of and requirements for a matching mechanism and then goes on to discuss the technical aspects in more detail.

A matching tool should not be designed with self-interest as the dominant perspective and thus include only asylum seekers who are highly qualified. The experience gained from the matching tool of the relocation programme that failed after its introduction in 2015 indicates that particular attention must be paid to how the list of criteria is formulated. The formulation and weighting of the criteria should be developed democratically and transparently rather than technocratically. It is therefore important that different perspectives and interests are taken into account – in particular, the views of refugees themselves. Greater weight should be given to fundamental criteria such as language skills and the ties of family and friends. Criteria that violate the EU's anti-discrimination directive are unacceptable. For example, it should not be possible to express a preference for a particular religion, or any other group-specific characteristic.

Furthermore, preferences should not be formulated in an overly restrictive way. For example, if a community formulates a preference for families, this can indirectly mean that single men without a family are excluded. To prevent this, such criteria could be formulated as offers – for example, offers of places in kindergartens or schools to prevent the closure of classes. The advantage of matching at a local rather than a national level is the increased probability of matches being identified for both sides. For instance, there are certainly municipalities that would like to welcome families with numerous children in order to keep their village school going (see the village of Golzow in Brandenburg), while others complain about a shortage of apprentices and would therefore want to receive young single men. In the same way, preferences for specific professions should not be included in the list of criteria. Instead, the focus should be on sectors facing a labour shortage. Instead of being able to set a preference for doctors, for example, this approach means asking refugees if they could and would be prepared to work in the health sector, because this covers a larger professional group (both high- and low-skilled workers as well as vocational trainees).

The biggest challenge for a matching system is ensuring that the number of available places is not dependent on the number of perfect matches, as that would give rise to a danger that the people who are easy to match will find a place and those who are more difficult to match will not. This problem could be reduced, although not completely eliminated, by allowing municipalities to make offers of reception and then allowing the asylum seekers themselves to decide which municipality to choose from among a number of matches. This would mean that a municipality could only prioritise certain criteria in advance and not select from among the asylum seekers after submitting its reception offer. This does, however, leave unanswered the question of who is then responsible for processing and receiving asylum seekers who do not obtain a match or who cannot participate in such a municipal reception market because they are highly vulnerable and in need of special protection. There is probably no way around a compulsory reception quota for vulnerable groups, but this could, for example, be accompanied by additional financial incentives. Nevertheless, this would still be an improvement on the current situation, in which the intention is to admit only the most vulnerable groups – for example, from the Greek camps – which means that everyone else currently has no prospect of moving to another EU member state.

How would such a matching mechanism work in practice? Once a basic set of criteria has been devised (including a clear hierarchy for the criteria), a questionnaire based on those criteria must be put together to compare the preferences of asylum seekers with those of municipalities and generate matches – that is, suitable pairings. The process is similar to the methods employed by dating apps (though their exact algorithms are closely guarded business secrets). The asylum seekers then select from among several matches with municipalities that appeal to them, thus achieving the flexibility required by both sides. For instance, it may be the case that a municipality has already been selected by other refugees.

The automated alignment of preferences and the resulting matches could be carried out within an app that would also allow municipalities to present themselves in more detail – for instance, in the form of a short video giving basic information about the municipality or a direct address to the newcomers. This could make it easier for asylum seekers to decide whether to choose a municipality. Once a municipality has been selected, it must also confirm the match.

The reconciliation of large amounts of data from municipalities and asylum seekers would need to be automated through algorithm-based methods. Aside from the algorithm developed by the European Asylum Support Office for the failed EU relocation programme, which is not openly available, there are now a number of further studies and pilot projects that have also developed matching algorithms for the resettlement of asylum seekers and vulnerable people. However, these come almost exclusively from international resettlement programmes (that is, the resettlement of vulnerable people from third countries to a destination country, often with the support of international organisations such as the International Organization for Migration and the UNHCR).[2] A team of researchers at Stanford University, for example, has developed an algorithm based on historical data specifically to move people to regions and cities that better match their job market profile and where they have a higher chance of finding employment.[3] However, this algorithm does not include the preferences of the asylum seekers themselves and defines the calculated probability of finding a job as the most important criterion for its matches. This algorithm is currently being tested in Switzerland with the aim of distributing as effectively as possible people who come to the country via the resettlement programme. In the pilot, half the people being resettled are randomly distributed among the cantons, while the remaining half are assigned to the canton that best fits their personal profile through use of the algorithm.

Another pilot project, called Annie MOORE, was launched in the United States in 2018; it uses a matching algorithm developed by the researchers Will Jones and Alexander Teytelboym.[4] Unlike the Stanford project, its objective is primarily to identify a good place within the United States to resettle those who have no family ties in the country. However, in this project the final decision on where people may settle is made by the administrators, rather than the asylum- and protection-seekers themselves.[5] In 2023 a further pilot project was launched in Germany, on behalf of German municipalities, to test whether a targeted distribution based on algorithms is superior to a random distribution.

A matching mechanism is thus already technically feasible, and examples and studies have already been devised and conducted. It is

---

2   This is in part because resettlement programmes are the subject of considerable international support, although their importance has declined considerably in recent years, and also because very detailed screening processes take place before leaving the third country, that is, prior to the "resettlement", whereas relocations concern people already inside the EU.

3   Bansak, K., J. Ferwerda, J. Hainmueller, A. Dillon, D. Hangartner, D. Lawrence and J. Weinstein (2018) "Improving refugee integration through data-driven algorithmic assignment". *Science*, 359(6373): 325–329.

4   Trapp, A., A. Teytelboym, A. Martinello, T. Andersson and N. Ahani (2020) "Placement optimization in refugee resettlement". Working paper 2018:23. Department of Economics, Lund University (http://project.nek.lu.se/publications/workpap/papers/wp18_23.pdf). See also the RefugeesAI website: www.refugees.ai.

5   Calamur, K. (2019) "How technology could revolutionize refugee resettlement". *The Atlantic*, 26 April (www.theatlantic.com/international/archive/2019/04/how-technology-could-revolutionize-refugee-resettlement/587383).

important, however, to ensure that the technical implementation of the matching process also takes into account the refugees' preferences (for cities over small towns, for example). Although the asylum seekers only get to choose between the offers of a few municipalities and thus do not have a truly free choice, it comes closer to the objective of freedom of movement than ignoring their wishes altogether and simply assigning them randomly to a country and a municipality – particularly when asylum seekers get relocated to communities that show no willingness to receive them and in which they do not feel welcome. Moreover, such a matching app could also be a decision-making aid, since asylum seekers often know only the general characteristics of certain EU member states and have no knowledge of their specific reception location.

2.5 Funding through a European Integration and Development Fund

I am therefore calling for more opportunities to be given to municipalities as the places where the voluntary reception of refugees and their social integration take place and must be supported. If their own interests are also to play a role (in order to achieve a win-win situation), then it makes sense to introduce a financial incentive system to ensure this. It would provide mayors, citizens' initiatives and companies with additional arguments in favour of starting such a process – including setting up "municipal development advisory boards" – while taking the wind out of the sails of the fearful and also of right-wing radicals, who generally oppose receiving refugees and claim that it would be at the expense of locals, and who thus whip up anti-democratic sentiment. In addition, many municipalities need not only more inhabitants but also financing for their projects.

So far, these financing needs have been met by national tax revenues and national and provincial governments. In addition, there are also longstanding and extensive EU programmes to which municipalities and cities can apply. But these generally have several drawbacks. Successfully applying for those programmes is complex and not really feasible for small and medium-sized municipalities. The funds are generally channelled through national governments, which keep a close watch over them for political reasons. This is a long and slow process, and there is often a sticking point somewhere along the way to the municipalities. Another problem is that granting such funds requires co-financing from the municipalities – a cost they are often unable to afford. Moreover, citizens do not even notice that the money that helps them comes from the EU. They are often critical of the EU without realising that it gives them a substantial helping hand.

One further problem of all such programmes, including those offered within member states, is that they allow little room for citizens to express their own ideas. This means that citizens face the difficulty of adapting their projects to the programmes' specifications, which hampers citizens' ability to participate in politics. If we wish to promote democratic participation, these financing programmes must earmark a portion of the funds for municipalities' and citizens' own initiatives, subject to only general guidelines. This process would, of course, require overarching political guidance.

Citizens would also acquire experience, thus putting representative democracy on a stronger social footing. The best way to decide which projects to finance within the municipalities is by conducting public debates in conjunction with the local development advisory boards. The incentives for municipalities to admit refugees would therefore also include the ability to draw up and implement projects of their own that are tailored to their local situations, in accordance with loose guidelines. All expenditure must, of course, be accounted for, as the funding is ultimately taxpayers' money.

This highlights the need to finance the reception of refugees from a European fund for "integration and communal development", which municipalities would be able to apply to directly for funding – if possible without having to go through the national level – and which would give them scope for their specific projects. Common sense would dictate that people with experience in municipalities should be involved in approving the financing, with stakeholder collaboration between politicians, organised civil society and companies. Such people are best able to assess the feasibility, originality and practicality of applications. Direct financing by Brussels has long been the goal of associations representing European cities.

Beyond the resettlement of refugees, it would also be a good way to weaken the grip exerted on cities and municipalities by national governments that are currently moving in an undemocratic and authoritarian direction. In contrast to their national governments, these municipalities often wish to uphold democracy and the rule of law, and the authoritarian governments in Hungary and Poland, for example, are therefore increasingly trying to starve them of funding.

For its part, the EU has in recent years consistently stressed the importance of cities and municipalities for European cohesion and for the development and implementation of new ideas. It has also cautiously presented direct financing programmes such as the Urban Innovation Action programme, which, among other things, promotes climate-friendly sustainability (through, for instance, the circular economy, saving energy and conserving resources) but also the integration of refugees. What we are proposing is, therefore, very much on trend, but it does require a strong and courageous political will – particularly because, when it comes to the refugee question, national (and especially conservative) governments are acting as a bloc, largely through legal arguments. This is precisely what has led to the inhumanity of European refugee policy.

In light of the practical conditions I have set out above for the funding of refugee admissions and financial incentives, I therefore propose a "European Fund for Integration and Local Development", to which the receiving municipalities can apply for financing to cover the costs of integrating refugees, and from which they would receive additional funding in the same amount for municipal projects that are in their own interests.

At the end of 2020, the Friedrich Ebert Stiftung in Brussels and Jens Geier, former rapporteur for the Progressive Alliance of Socialists and Democrats in the European Parliament, commissioned an expert opinion to examine the legal requirements for the establishment of such a fund. The opinion concluded that the fund would be possible without needing changes in the EU treaties, but it would require the will of the member states to get it off the ground.[6]

Two conditions, which are both functionally and politically important for the fund, would have to be dealt with pragmatically. Firstly, for legal reasons, the local government projects that are to be funded in addition to refugee integration would in some way need to be linked to the reception of refugees, although the funding would not have to be used for them directly. The conditions could also include encouraging the willingness of locals to receive refugees. Secondly, it is legally challenging to make the reception of refugees a condition for funding that also finances development benefitting locals.

We believe that pragmatic solutions can be found that meet both conditions. However, the adoption of the EU's seventh financial framework means that the time has now passed to apply for the establishment of such a fund. That means a wait of about four years until the next financial

---

6   Fontana, S. (2021) "Integrations- & Entwicklungsfonds".

framework is negotiated. This is no oversight, however, because the political will to explore new solutions has until now been lacking. We could make good use of the coming years to trial the most important elements of our strategy in order to see how they work in practice and, if necessary, adjust them so that the fund could finally be established in the next financial framework. Reforms, particularly in the international sphere, often take place in stages – in other words, incrementally.

It would therefore be appropriate to estimate the number of refugees who need to be rescued from their current misery, as well as those whose right to asylum is likely to need reexamination in the next few years. This is the only way to at least roughly quantify the amount of funding that will need to be raised to trial the strategy. This is a transitional or preparatory strategy that we would need to expand in the coming years, in advance of moving to the European Fund for Integration and Local Development, which would have to be set up in the next financial framework.

*

According to the UNHCR, some 461,000 people sought asylum in the EU in 2020, of which about 150,000 were granted refugee status.[7]

Estimates put the number of people currently living in difficult and sometimes inhumane conditions in the overcrowded camps in Greece and the Balkans, without active asylum procedures, at around 200,000. Their misery is clearly intended to deter other refugees. Some are still waiting to commence their asylum procedure; others are awaiting the processing of their application, and others have seen theirs rejected.

The EU committed itself to receiving around 30,000 people in 2021 through the UNHCR Resettlement Programme. Around 2,000 refugees are being held in inhumane conditions in camps in Libya; realistically, they would need to be brought to the EU via a separate resettlement programme. Moreover, the UNHCR stated that fulfilling the key priorities would require an EU-wide resettlement target of 70,000 refugees in 2020 and 80,000 refugees in 2021, which makes a total of 150,000 for the two years.[8]

The total figure for those who would need to be provided for directly was around 685,000 in 2021. The UNHCR documented 461,000 asylum seekers in Europe in 2020, and if we add the 150,000 receiving regular

---

7   "Asylum trends 2020 preliminary overview", European Asylum Support Office (www.easo.europa.eu/asylum-trends-2020-preliminary-overview).

8   UNHCR (2020) "To the European Union: resettlement needs and key priorities for 2021". UNHCR recommendations (www.unhcr.org/en-us/publications/euroseries/5fb7e43a4/unhcr-recommendations-european-unionresettlement-needs-key-priorities.html).

care and also the 150,000 whose applications were rejected but who could not be returned, the result is a figure of just under 850,000 people who would have to be cared for under this proposal.

The European Union has about 450 million inhabitants, so this figure would amount to less than 0.25% of the population. After World War II, Germany, then largely in ruins, had about 65 million inhabitants. Of these, around 14 million people had fled from its former eastern provinces, accounting for some 20% of the population.

The European Union has pledged around €10,000 per person as an annual contribution for relocation. For 850,000 people, this would amount to €8.5 billion per year. If municipal investments were made at the same level as the integration costs per person, this would add a further €8.5 billion to the cost. A European Fund for Integration and Local Development would therefore require funding of approximately €20 billion if we include the additional costs over and above the minimum of the annual €10,000 per person to be integrated. As previously stated, half of this would be used for municipal investments unrelated to refugees.

The question is whether a fund could first be set up for a preparatory strategy by reallocating some of the budget for migration; this fund would correspond in principle to the envisaged integration and development fund.

A construct such as the EU Emergency Trust Fund for Africa, which was established in 2013, might also be a possibility for a coalition of municipalities willing to receive refugees, as set out in the following section. But setting up any such fund will require political will.

2.6 "Enhanced cooperation" or a "coalition of the willing"?

Our alternative – namely, a *humane* refugee policy – aims to replace the obligatory solidarity that has so far been demanded of all EU member states with voluntary cooperation between those willing to receive refugees. This involves a change of perspective, with refugees no longer seen as simply a burden to be avoided wherever possible or rejected altogether. Rather, they would be regarded as welcome fellow residents, with whom we wish to live and shape our future for the benefit of all (a win-win situation). The current legal situation requires a number of EU member states to be prepared to work together on the following strategy.

To create a reliable decentralised settlement system for asylum seekers in the EU, and thus to realistically set up effective, humane asylum procedures, these states must commit themselves to receiving a fixed quota of refugees. (The failure to "distribute" asylum seekers and those entitled to asylum in the EU is the main obstacle that has prevented a humane refugee policy for years.) The states should first determine which municipalities and cities within their jurisdiction are prepared to receive which allocations of refugees. Following a matching process, refugees would then be sent to those municipalities and cities with the help of national and local institutions. If the numbers that municipalities are prepared to receive are fewer than the allocated quota, the cooperating states would undertake, as a sort of "safety net", to admit those remaining, in accordance with a pre-agreed formula. They would coordinate closely in the asylum process and agree on common standards. (See the next chapter for further details.)

In principle, two forms of voluntary cooperation between European member states are conceivable.

"Enhanced cooperation" under Article 328 of the Treaty on the Functioning of the European Union

"Enhanced cooperation" is one of the ways in which the EU provides for gradual integrated cooperation. It must be authorised by the European Council and the European Parliament following a proposal from the Commission. Other examples of graduated integration procedures for European cooperation are the Schengen Agreement and the European Monetary Union, which are based on other legal foundations. Whether they come to fruition depends on the political will of the member states. In any case, there are no fundamental legal obstacles to them doing so. Such pioneering initiatives have become models throughout the world for initiating political innovations between multiple cooperating states.

A minimum of nine states must participate in enhanced cooperation. The European Parliament must first agree to it, and a two-thirds majority is then sufficient to approve it in the European Council. The project must be financed by the participating states. The Council may decide otherwise only unanimously. As with the reconstruction fund, a sense of imagination would not be amiss here. Enhanced cooperation would fulfil a task – the task of admitting people seeking asylum or protection in Europe – that the EU states should already be fulfilling and to which they have committed themselves in international conventions (see Chapter 1.4). With the agreement of the European Council, the Commission could devise and implement financial incentive schemes that support enhanced cooperation. Since the framework of enhanced cooperation would not oblige Council members to participate in the reception of refugees, it is conceivable that they would be more likely to approve such a scheme (which would require only two-thirds support rather than the current unanimity) than they are to vote in favour of obligatory solidarity arrangements for the reception of refugees that are binding on all states. Furthermore, it is not in asylum seekers' interests to be admitted by member states that are strongly opposed to admitting them. If they do not wish to show solidarity and take part in the scheme, nonparticipating member states should contribute financially to the reception and integration of the arrivals, instead of contributing only to the funding of external border controls. Those border-control costs would, however, also be significantly reduced by a new asylum and refugee policy that creates legal and safe ways of entering Europe. This is a topic I will return to.

With such a proposal, there are also chances that a well-conceived asylum and refugee policy might strengthen democracy in states such as Poland and Hungary, which are currently sliding into authoritarianism. States that do not want to receive asylum seekers would be relieved of this obligation by enhanced cooperation between willing states. This would be an argument for contributing towards the financial burden of enhanced cooperation in receiving asylum seekers. Of course, the Commission's proposal for a European policy on refugees and asylum in September 2020 has already muddied the waters here, because it maintains the fiction of obligatory solidarity for all without actually demanding it from the member states.

Furthermore, by directly financing municipalities, the EU could set in motion a political dynamic to strengthen the rule of law (a dynamic already partly underway through the European Court of Justice's legal oversight mechanism and through linking EU financing to rule-of-law criteria for the recipient country, in line with the budget decision in summer 2020). This is because the additional financing of receiving municipalities acts as a considerable draw for many cities and towns, particularly in the Visegrád states. Municipalities within countries currently ruled by authoritarian governments might also demand to participate in the financing mechanism. In Poland, for example, 17 cities publicly declared in a 2017 manifesto that they wished to take part in admitting migrants, because of – among other things – labour shortages in economically up-and-coming cities such as Gdańsk, Warsaw and Poznan. They might demand that their government participate in enhanced cooperation, thereby giving new life to the EU's human rights and international obligations

A "coalition of the willing"

A "coalition of the willing" to receive refugees would be less clearly regulated by law. The term has generally been used in the context of participation in military operations, and the 2003 Iraq war in particular. This designation was also used to describe one-off activities during Christmas 2020, such as the reception of children and young people from the disastrous situation of the burned-out Moria camp on the island of Lesbos in Greece. Ska Keller, leader of the Greens/European Free Alliance group in the EU parliament, used the phrase in autumn 2020 to describe a longer-term refugee policy, because she suspected that the Commission's forthcoming proposal for a new refugee policy would not only fail to bring about a humane solution but would also solidify the inhumane general direction of the EU's refugee policy towards a "Fortress Europe" approach.

To date, the term has not been used in the context of the humane regulation of European refugee and asylum policy beyond ad hoc measures. Its advantage is that the conditions for such a coalition are not formally defined in the same way as they are for enhanced cooperation. The downside is that such measures cannot claim to be a binding Europe-wide refugee policy unless the European Parliament and the Council were to agree on this format instead of the Commission's failed proposal of September 2020.

A coalition of the willing could be regulated in the same way as enhanced cooperation. There would, however, be no minimum number of participating states. That said, at least five or six states would need to be involved if it were to be perceived even as merely the nucleus of a European policy and to be able to cope with the task at hand. This would be a realistic prospect if the EU were to furnish such a coalition with financial incentives. One of the shortcomings of the Commission's 2020 initiative on European asylum policy is that it put forward no positive incentives to admit refugees, as doing so would mean that the European Union would have to recognise that its current lowest common denominator – strengthening its defences against refugees at the EU's external borders – is a morally self-contradictory one. It is a self-contradiction that undermines the EU's future, and the coalition of the willing outlined above is the only proposition that offers the chance to escape from the impasse of European inhumanity. Overcoming this will require a great deal of public pressure. This book is intended to serve that purpose. If a strategy is legally and politically feasible, relies on voluntary action and benefits all parties concerned, there is a chance that the public will get behind such a sensible policy. It would only be opposed by those who see the chance of using the festering sore of an inhumane refugee policy as a way of whipping up hatred in our democracies, such as Viktor Orbán and radical right-wing parties such as Alternative für Deutschland (AfD).

In addition to Germany under a non-conservative government, it is conceivable that France, Luxembourg and the southern countries of first entry would in future participate in this process. The coalition would need to be open to other member states and could publicly demonstrate the benefits and attractiveness of this strategy. It would also be a decisive act of solidarity towards the countries of first entry at the southern and eastern external borders of Europe, including Bulgaria and Hungary.

3 | Access to humane asylum procedures in Europe

3.1 Overcoming the deterrence approach

Before I set out the key points of a humane European asylum procedure below, it is necessary to formulate a prerequisite for its success (which I also briefly addressed at the start of the book): a humane approach to asylum procedures – including accommodating and caring for the applicants during the procedures – presupposes that we reject once and for all the fundamental notion of deterring refugees as "annoying disruptors" of our normal lives. This unspoken but easily identifiable premise is behind many of the political decisions of the EU and the individual nation states. Continuing to abide by the guiding principle of deterring refugees and by the objective of preventing as many of them as possible from reaching the continent will sabotage debate around any sensible approach to asylum procedures and surreptitiously undermine such an approach in practice. The fact that the principle of deterrence is not merely a "reasonable" limitation on the numbers of refugees to be admitted – however "reasonable" could be defined – is demonstrated by the persistence of this motif of deterrence even when the numbers of refugees and asylum seekers fall significantly. This means that, if we are unable to achieve a fundamental cultural shift on this issue, we will end up in a downward spiral of deterrence and externalisation of costs.

In addition to the aforementioned motive for whipping up fear and anger through anti-migration propaganda, many people whose prime interest is deterrence are afraid that a humane asylum and refugee policy would "open the floodgates" and bring all the world's refugees, or at least all the African ones, to Europe or Germany. This is referred to by the term "pull factor". I will deal with this very influential and widespread objection to overcoming the inhumane status quo after this chapter.

Having taken note of these concerns, the European Union has increasingly formulated and pursued an asylum and refugee policy whose primary aim is to halt or intercept refugees wherever possible outside the borders of the EU, contrary to the international and human rights obligations it has entered into. Reports from the interior ministers of the nation states, who perceive refugees first and foremost as threats to internal security, usually focus on reducing the number of incoming asylum seekers rather than on successful inclusion and integration.

For many years this has resulted in repeated attempts to carry out asylum procedures outside the EU and to return as many refugees as possible from the EU's external borders. To secure access to European asylum procedures and structure them humanely, the first step must therefore be to identify where they can and should take place.

3.2 Centralised European asylum procedures

Locations for centralised procedures in European assessment centres

All attempts to establish assessment centres outside the EU – in North Africa, for example – or to define them as "extraterritorial" have so far failed and will continue to fail. Not only do these initiatives require North African and Middle Eastern countries to set up border camps against their own interests, they also undermine fruitful cooperation with those countries – cooperation that is necessary to achieve a satisfactory approach to refugee policy and migration (including the necessity of returns) and an improved relationship with Africa. Even simply leaving the question open of whether such assessment centres should be located within the EU or elsewhere is sure to result in a failure to identify a solution. This is an issue on which we need to find the courage to make a decision.

The locations for such asylum procedures can only be within the EU. As explained above, if countries are to allow them on their territory, it is necessary – once the procedures have been completed – that there be a reliable approach for the subsequent decentralised reception of people entitled to asylum or to residence (subsidiary protection) and also of those who, for whatever reason, cannot be returned. We have put together proposals for this. At the same time, there must be rules around the return of those who are not entitled to remain. That is something we also cannot turn a blind eye to.

These new European assessment centres must not be overcrowded like those on the Greek islands. That would be inhumane, and no country is going to voluntarily allow such "hotspots" on its territory. The EU should have several locations in different European countries – and not only in the southern countries of first entry – where asylum and residence claims can be assessed in accordance with common European law. Refugees would be taken from their landing location to one of the assessment centres by the national or European authorities in accordance with pragmatic criteria (such as geographical proximity, occupancy rate and the refugees' preference).

If, as I propose, we rely to the greatest possible extent on a voluntary approach and positive incentives as a way of ensuring the reliability of decentralised reception following the examination procedures – both on the part of the refugees and on the part of the receiving municipalities – and wish to regulate decentralised reception via a matching system, the location of the initial asylum procedure is of minor importance because it does not determine the eventual place of residence.

Indispensable elements of humane asylum procedures in European assessment centres: transparency, fairness, trustworthiness, swiftness

What would humane asylum procedures look like? Who should carry them out? How long should they be allowed to take? How can the refugees' stay in the assessment centres be used in their interests so that they remain there voluntarily during the assessment process? How can a repetition of the inhumane conditions in the previous hotspots be avoided?

First of all, the question of whether the Dublin III Regulation should be maintained, which was addressed by the Commission proposal of September 2020, needs to be clarified. In my opinion, the answer to that question is "definitely not". Not only are the current Dublin Convention and the Dublin III Regulation frequently undermined, they also lead to time-consuming, paradoxical and above all costly transfer requests and procedures, and cause insecurity among the refugees. Furthermore, they fail to respond to the legitimate demands for solidarity being made by the main countries of first entry in Southern and Eastern Europe, which are calling for the costs and complexity of assessment procedures and temporary accommodation to be spread among all European countries. Having examined the European Parliament's 2020 evaluation of this situation, we reached the following conclusions.

To ensure that the assessment procedures are humane, it is particularly important that they are as transparent and fair as possible. This engenders trust and speeds up the process, which benefits both sides.

The Dutch procedure and the Swiss approach (which is based on the Dutch one) provide practical examples of this. A crucial factor is that citizens' initiatives such as refugee organisations must have immediate access to the assessment centres so they can help the refugees and ensure transparency. Just as importantly, applicants must be granted independent personal legal advice from the outset.

This benefits all those involved. It saves time, because all the information and documents required for the asylum procedure are collected and processed immediately in a professional manner. It creates trust on all sides and prevents false expectations. In Germany, the current system makes it difficult for refugees to access legal assistance, particularly for those in the so-called *AnkER-Zentren*,[1] or "anchor centres", as lawyers and civil society initiatives to support refugees are often not allowed access to them. In the Netherlands, such access is an indispensable element of the speedy, transparent transfer of information.

As a result, fewer decisions are appealed in the Dutch asylum procedure than in the German. This both indicates that asylum is granted fairly rather than restrictively and avoids unnecessary procedures. The fact that there are so many successful appeals in Germany clearly indicates that Germany's Federal Office for Migration and Refugees (BAMF), which is responsible for the assessments, is not conducting them sufficiently fairly and reliably. That is why the option of statutory revision is indispensable. But would it not be more beneficial for all the parties concerned if the procedures were conducted from the very outset in a manner that resulted in carefully considered outcomes, obviating the need for unnecessary procedures? The example of the Netherlands shows that transparency and justice are in everyone's interests, benefiting the refugees and, at the same time, avoiding unnecessary costs for the host country. Our entire proposal for a humane asylum and refugee policy is based on this philosophy of creating win-win situations.

Nonetheless, even in the Netherlands, much depends on the influence the government has on the country's asylum procedures. When the country's right-wing liberals under Prime Minister Rutte wished to restrict legal assistance, they were publicly challenged with the argument that such a provision would extend asylum procedures and would thus be detrimental to the Netherlands. Rutte's proposal was yet one more based on the motive of deterrence.

---

1 *Ankunkft, Entscheidung and Rückfuhrung Zentren*; that is, arrival, decision and repatriation centres.

Ensuring that assessment centres do not become prisons: structured stay and practical support for refugees

The Dutch asylum procedures also teach us that it is in the interests of all parties that the refugees' initial accommodation period is well structured and allows them to use their time there in a way that is beneficial to them. That is the best way to ensure that they remain there by choice, as having no purpose and no say in your life is a depressing experience for anyone. For young people who have fled alone, in particular, a lack of direction and no say in what happens to them gives rise to feelings of frustration and can lead to them going astray.

In the Netherlands, a distinction is made between those phases that are intended for recuperation after a strenuous journey and those that are to be used in preparing for the asylum assessment. In our proposal for setting up a matching system between refugees and the municipalities that wish to admit them, refugees would be able to use any remaining waiting time to examine the reception offers of willing communities and, where appropriate, to contact those that seem interesting. This could be organised by representatives of the municipalities or civil society. Such an approach could lead to smoother future procedures for subsequent settlement in the EU, which would be to the benefit of all.

When refugees are forced to spend extended periods in primary reception centres, the question arises of whether these centres do not, in effect, become prisons for those whose applications take longer to process. This in turn raises the question of whether to make "investments" (for example, in the form of language courses or training courses) in refugees who have yet to be allocated a final country of residence. This is a question that should be examined in more detail: activities such as apprenticeships in companies – which really only make sense if they lead to a recognised qualification and can then benefit the companies offering them – are certainly problematic when a refugee's future remains uncertain, particularly if the company has invested money but is unable to benefit from its investment. Such training, however, is definitely an advantage for the refugees themselves and may also be beneficial for the internal security of the country in which the assessment centre is located, as it allows young people to put their otherwise unused energies into constructive activities. This is especially true of activities such as academic education and language courses, because they offer transferable skills. Leisure activities – sports, crafts, cultural activities – are also suitable and can make coercive measures superfluous.

The costs for the host centres or institutions must be shared on a European basis, as the reception institutions do not generally benefit in a direct or tangible way from this expenditure. They will, however, reap the benefits of their generosity in the long term, while also reducing the short-term costs of internal security, particularly if constructive solutions are employed.

The duration of stay in such centres should not exceed three months, including any appeal processes. It is necessary to empirically determine whether centralised solutions are sufficient to guarantee a humane environment. In instances of the procedures dragging on for more than three months, the refugees would need to be moved from centralised to decentralised reception centres.

Different categories of refugees: immigration and employment arrangements must be complementary

But what about those who have no prospect of having their claim recognised? Will they not just leave the assessment centres and go underground?

At this point, we must introduce a distinction between different categories of refugees, in part so we can find more appropriate – that is, fairer – solutions. As the term "economic refugees" suggests (a term that has negative connotations in Germany and elsewhere and should be replaced by the term "migrant workers"), there are very different reasons for seeking refuge, and a humane approach demands that these differences be duly taken into account. There are also differences in meaning between colloquial and legal categories. Refugees can be

(1) people who have a right to asylum in the EU following an application in accordance with the provisions of the Universal Declaration of Human Rights, the Geneva Convention, EU asylum law and the European Convention on Human Rights as described in Chapter 1.4;
(2) people with subsidiary protection who cannot claim asylum but may not be deported;
(3) people who may legally be deported but whose deportation is not possible for various reasons ("tolerated persons");
(4) people who are unable to live in their country of origin for reasons not provided for in asylum law (such as disasters; internal, but not state, persecution; and a lack of livelihood due to climate change);

(5) people who are seeking better opportunities for themselves or their family or village community (labour migration) because they see no prospects in their country of origin and who often provide that country with more financial support through their remittances than international aid organisations;

(6) people who, for legal reasons, can and must be returned.

Our proposals focus on refugees under the Geneva Convention, those with subsidiary protection and those who cannot be returned but have no right to asylum. However, since refugees do not in reality arrive in Europe sorted into neat categories and, moreover, new reasons for fleeing have emerged in recent decades that imperil people's lives in their home countries, we must consider all those who arrive at an assessment centre for asylum seekers and at least outline proposals for ensuring them a humane environment. These cannot be precise legal provisions; they can only define the political challenges that need to be addressed.

Opponents of a humane refugee policy often justify their hostility by stating that most refugees come to Europe "only" for the economic benefits and not because of state persecution. While it is not possible to address in more detail the complex reasons for their seeking asylum, the objection raises the challenge of relieving the burden on asylum assessment centres by giving other options and ways to reach their destination to people who set out on refugee routes for reasons that clearly do not conform with asylum law but that are nonetheless perfectly understandable and legitimate from a humane perspective.[2]

In consequence, a humane refugee policy needs an immigration policy or the possibility of (even temporary) work permits. Asylum procedures will only be significantly relieved if the EU or EU states offer alternative methods of lawful access, thus giving people alternative, more promising ways to get to Europe. As long as this is not the case, it will, realistically, remain necessary to meticulously check all arrivals in order to ascertain whether they are eligible for asylum.

Attempts by the EU and national interior ministers to ease the burden on asylum procedures by means of simplified "preliminary assessments" that quickly "filter out" people who "obviously" do not qualify for protection through asylum are ineffectual. Such attempts always amount to

---

2 Expert Commission on the Causes of Flight (2021) "Krisen vorbeugen, Perspektiven schaffen, Menschen schützen". Report of the Federal Government of Germany's Expert Commission on the Causes of Flight (Fachkommission Fluchtursachen), April.

restricting the right to asylum by failing to carry out a thorough assessment of individual cases. The most appropriate way of relieving the pressure on the asylum system is to offer refugees alternatives.

Refugees who are not legally entitled to asylum and do not enjoy subsidiary protection but cannot be returned for whatever reason are a source of particular controversy. A political decision must be reached for such cases. A category should be introduced for such people that avoids them going underground, which represents a bad outcome for both sides. This requires finding unconventional arrangements that avoid endless pointless journeys by refugees and costly legal proceedings. A pragmatic way of dealing with such cases can be found in the Netherlands: in 2007, the government and the municipalities agreed on a "general pardon", which allowed 26,000 people to "regularise" their status.[3]

Transfer, return and offers

Once the asylum procedure has been completed, refugees should not simply be released or ejected from the European assessment centre without being given further opportunities and social protection. Those with the right to asylum or to subsidiary protection should be able to move as soon as possible to the municipality that can receive them in accordance with the matching system. This municipality would be expected to meet the refugees' basic needs – housing, work or training, education, healthcare, subsistence costs, social and cultural integration – and to help them transition to living independently.

Those refugees who, without a right to asylum, have only a temporary leave to remain must also be given opportunities – for example, to start work or enter education for the indeterminate period of their stay in the EU. Financial incentives could be offered to municipalities to cover the costs of such measures, as an inducement to receive refugees under such hard-to-quantify conditions.

Returning those who cannot claim the right to asylum is the most difficult obstacle to a humane refugee policy, but it is one we cannot ignore. One important caveat, however, must first be considered: under the banner of deterring refugees, both the EU and its member states have in recent years declared an increasing number of countries to be

---

3 Thränhardt, D. (2016) *Asylverfahren in den Niederlanden* (Gütersloh: Bertelsmann Stiftung), p. 12 (www.bertelsmann-stiftung.de/fileadmin/files/Projekte/28_Einwanderu ng_und_Vielfalt/IB_Studie_ Asylverfahren_NL_Thraenhardt_2016.pdf).

"safe countries of origin" that could not be considered as such either in general or for specific individuals (such as LGBTQ people). They have also applied criteria for the return of refugees that are not credible. To increase the number of safe countries of origin as much as possible, they have often taken as a basis the percentage of asylum applications from those countries' nationals that were refused in the past, even though this statistic bears little relation to the current state of those countries or the dangers faced by specific individuals. A striking example of this is declaring Afghanistan to be a safe country of origin – a classification that is often vehemently disputed by those with knowledge of the situation on the ground.

Nevertheless, while migrants have no alternative way to enter Europe other than applying for asylum, there will always be a need for returns, and these can be facilitated by supporting their journey back. A humane refugee policy should also include a balanced immigration/migration policy, as described, for example, in the UN Global Compact for Migration.

3.3 Decentralised national procedures in individual European nation states

Another possibility would be to relocate those claiming asylum before commencing the procedures, but with mandatory registration and a matching procedure. By managing relocation through the matching tool while simultaneously creating legal certainty for those seeking asylum, this approach would address the concerns of the EU member states with only internal borders because access to the asylum procedure would be guaranteed and responsibility would be definitively established. This would also relieve the EU's external border states from being responsible for the majority of asylum procedures. While asylum seekers would still not enjoy freedom of movement within Europe as EU citizens do, it would still improve their situation since – in contrast to compulsory relocation – their preferences as to their eventual place of residence would be taken into account and they would be given a choice, albeit a limited one, about where to settle.

To ensure that the relocation to municipalities is not tied to acceptance rates in asylum procedures, participating member states would have to focus even more than at present on complying with the legally binding standards set out in the Asylum Procedures, Reception and Qualification Directives. A fundamental principle of the rule of law is that decisions taken by public bodies can be subjected to judicial review.

This also applies to asylum law: decisions to grant or refuse asylum or international protection must be judicially reviewable. In other words, the parties concerned must be able to appeal against a decision. These legal remedies are currently available only at the national level. This means that Europe's common legal standards must be strengthened if decentralised reception by municipalities is to succeed. The European Union Agency for Asylum (EUAA) could play a larger role, but that would require it to be more accountable and transparent.[4]

The Malta mechanism provides one possible template for how decentralised voluntary reception could be organised in Europe in terms of the specific procedural steps and the participation of European agencies and national authorities (more on this in the next section). Another possible template is the decentralised reception practised by Germany prior to the tightening of its asylum law between 2015 and 2017. Following a brief arrival phase, asylum seekers are relocated to the municipalities and, ideally, accommodated there in a decentralised manner. The big difference in the proposal set out here is that European municipalities would be receiving asylum seekers voluntarily, rather than being obliged to, as was the case in Germany. The asylum procedure would be conducted in a branch office of the national asylum authority, which means that asylum seekers would have to travel to that office for their hearing. Decentralised reception by municipalities gives asylum seekers better opportunities for participation in the community and ensures that the time spent awaiting a decision is not perceived as wasted. In addition, municipalities prepared to receive asylum seekers can put in place a welcoming infrastructure by cooperating with volunteer initiatives, refugee councils, established civil society organisations and an experienced public administration to facilitate their arrival.

What takes place where? From registration to decentralised procedures

Since the vast majority of asylum seekers have no legal way to enter the Schengen area or more specifically one of its member states in order to claim international protection, their entry is unauthorised; they simply

---

4 Proposals to strengthen transparency and accountability – such as those from the European Council on Refugees and Exiles – include having the executive director appointed cooperatively by the European Council, the European Commission and the European Parliament; obliging the EUAA to cooperate more closely with the Parliament; and increasing the representation of independent experts and NGOs on the board.

---

arrive somewhere – on Greece's Aegean islands, for example, or on the Spanish Canary Islands or the Italian island of Lampedusa. At these locations there are no border controls such as those found in airports or at motorway border posts.

The challenge for asylum seekers is to lodge a claim for asylum with a public authority and to gain access to the asylum procedure, while the EU member states are confronted with the need to ascertain who and how many have found their way to these places. At the same time, reception and housing facilities are in short supply in most of these arrival locations, particularly on the islands and along the Balkan route. It is therefore best if people do not have to remain in these places for any length of time. This becomes particularly apparent when the number of arrivals increases.

Incentives must therefore be created to encourage asylum seekers to voluntarily go to a preliminary reception centre instead of setting out on their own or going underground. This can happen only if they expect a fair asylum procedure and eventual relocation, rather than being forced to stay in the centre for an indefinite period. This also means learning from the failed hotspot approach and sharing responsibility for all the people going through the asylum procedure rather than preclassifying asylum seekers into different categories (as happens in "fast-track procedures" such as those on the Greek islands, or in so-called pre-examination or border procedures).[5]

The member states on the arrival routes can only be relied on to set up reception facilities if they can be sure that another member state will quickly assume responsibility for conducting the asylum procedures and for housing, caring for and, where necessary, returning the arrivals. A similar method of sharing responsibility was attempted under the Malta Declaration on the reception and relocation of those rescued at sea. Even though this procedure had its shortcomings,[6] it represents the

---

5   See Hänsel, V., and B. Kasparek (2020) "Hotspot-Lager als Blaupause für die Reform des Gemeinsamen Europäischen Asylsystems? Politikfolgenabschatzung des Hotspot-Ansatzes in Griechenland". Expert opinion produced on behalf of the Rat für Migration e.V. (Council for Migration), May.

6   A number of legitimate criticisms may be levelled at the Malta Declaration. Firstly, it applied only to arrivals in the central Mediterranean and not to those arriving at other sea and land borders (a point that Spain, Bulgaria and Greece have strongly criticised), and secondly, it has problematic elements around sea rescues; see the Amnesty International declaration on the return of rescue vessels to Libya: www.amnesty.org/en/latest/news/2019/10/eu-governments-face-crucial-decision-on-shared-sea-rescue-responsibility-2/.

first attempt in Europe to share the burden between a voluntary group of member states in a spirit of solidarity, following the failure of the previous relocation programme (2015–2017) and an obligatory quota due to a lack of will on the part of the European Council to enforce them and a lack of solidarity on the part of the member states.

The Malta Declaration was signed in Valletta on 23 September 2019 by Germany, France, Italy and Malta.[7] The declaration includes a mechanism for relocating those rescued at sea to other EU member states that have no maritime border in the central Mediterranean. Although only four countries officially signed the declaration, nine other member states participated in receiving the arrivals (Portugal, Luxembourg, Ireland, Spain, Finland, Lithuania, Bulgaria, Romania and Slovenia), according to the European Commission.[8] These member states come closest to a "coalition of the willing". The aim of the declaration was to rapidly relocate those rescued at sea within a period of no more than four weeks. The declaration was temporary in nature and has been suspended since March 2020, when the global Covid-19 pandemic started.

The standard procedure for the relocation of asylum seekers provided for in the declaration envisages four phases. The first phase focuses on identification and registration, health checks, and security checks.[9] The second phase is devoted to the transfer of asylum seekers from the country of first entry to the host state. The EUAA supports this by identifying vulnerabilities, links to family members in the EU, and linguistic and other cultural links to EU member states, as well as by using a matching algorithm to suggest admission to a member state other than the country of first entry. In the third phase the suggested member state then agrees or refuses to admit the asylum seeker and informs the EUAA, the European Commission and the member state of first entry. If the suggested member state agrees, the asylum procedure is then transferred to that country in accordance with the Dublin III Regulation under Article 17(2) (see the section in Chapter 1.4 of this book on the options for transfer

---

7   "Joint declaration of intent on a controlled emergency procedure – voluntary commitments by member states for a predictable temporary solidarity mechanism", 23 September 2019, Valletta, Malta (www.statewatch.org/media/documents/news/2019/sep/eu-temporary-voluntary-relocation-mechanism-declaration.pdf).

8   See the Commission's response to a question from the European Parliament: "The Malta declaration of 23 September 2019 and relocations" (www.europarl.europa.eu/doceo/document/E-9-2020-004456_EN.html).

9   In practice, it is the intensive security checks that delay rapid reception by another member state. It must be ensured that these do not lead to a form of disguised "cherry-picking" by setting overly strict criteria prior to relocation.

within the Dublin system), although the individual concerned may also object to the transfer of the asylum procedure. In the fourth phase the asylum seeker's relocation to the suggested member state is prepared and – sometimes with support from the International Organization for Migration – carried out.

A similar arrival phase, which should also last no longer than four weeks, could be combined with the matching system at the municipal level. During this phase, matches between asylum seekers and municipalities would be organised and asylum seekers could decide which municipality and member state they would like to move to. This means that asylum seekers wishing to submit an asylum application (category 1) would be registered in the Eurodac database in a preliminary reception centre along the arrival routes during the arrival phase. This serves to establish their identity and ensure that a procedure is initiated to examine their claim for asylum. Registration under category 1 allows asylum to be claimed, but the responsibility for examining the asylum request can also be transferred to another member state. A health check can also be carried out in the preliminary accommodation facility. This check should be associated with access to therapists, since many of those arriving will have been traumatised by the experience of fleeing and being displaced. With the support of the EUAA, vulnerability, individual characteristics and preferences would be fed into the matching platform and, based on an algorithm, available offers from municipalities would be compared with asylum seekers' preferences (see above). The member states that are willing to receive asylum seekers would guarantee that they will take on the asylum procedures for those individuals voluntarily received by their municipalities. After being presented with their matches, asylum seekers would have a week to choose a municipality or to lodge an appeal and have their asylum application procedure conducted in their country of first entry. If the municipal match is accepted, the authorities in the country of first entry will transfer the matched individual to the selected municipality – that is, to their relocation destination. Alternatively, this could also be done by issuing laissez-passer papers, which would allow asylum seekers to simply book a flight or buy a train ticket themselves to travel to the host municipality.

What happens during the procedures?

Once the asylum seekers arrive in the municipality, the settling-in process can start. Ideally, asylum seekers will be housed in the municipality in a decentralised manner, rather than in large-scale communal accommodation. In cities where housing is scarce, this will require finding innovative solutions. The city of Utrecht, for example, with the help of direct EU funding, has created a cultural centre to house asylum seekers that also offers affordable housing for young Utrechters.[10]

Asylum seekers would then have to travel to a national asylum authority office for their initial asylum procedure hearing. One way to ensure that they receive independent legal counsel on the procedure would be to set this out as a criterion for the matching process. Municipalities that voluntarily register to receive asylum seekers should therefore ensure in advance that there are lawyers and civil society organisations in their community or nearby that can accompany asylum seekers during the procedure. The journey to the hearing could be organised by the municipality, or alternatively the network or community sponsoring the individual's admission could organise the journey with private support. Asylum seekers are more likely to encounter support structures in municipalities where the authorities and residents have actively chosen to receive asylum seekers than in those that have asylum seekers allocated to them by a mandatory quota.

To speed up their participation in the social, economic and political life of the municipality, asylum seekers should not be prevented from working during the procedure. Integrating asylum seekers into the labour market gives them economic independence and makes it easier for municipalities to take them in, as it reduces the financial costs for the municipality. From the outset, asylum seekers should be ensured access to services that facilitate arrival and participation in the community, such as language courses and volunteers who help them to navigate the obligations required by public authorities. Their provision should not be linked to conditions such as the likelihood of a positive outcome to the asylum procedure.

Key elements and challenges

This potential approach builds on procedures already in place in the EU but relies much more on the willingness of municipalities to accept asylum seekers. The greater involvement of municipalities does, however, bring with it some specific challenges.

Municipalities would sometimes take in people who are not be granted protection at the end of the asylum procedure and who are therefore

---

10   See the Plan Einstein project: www.uia-initiative.eu/sites/default/files/2018-07/Plan%20Einstein%20Folder_ENG.pdf.

unlikely to receive a residence permit. This is already the case, but if we are to increase municipalities' willingness to receive asylum seekers, we must ensure that the expectations of both the municipalities and the asylum seekers are made explicit in advance. This is because municipalities face the challenge that they might take in people who ultimately cannot remain there permanently, despite having been a successful match. It is therefore very important to take the pressure off the asylum process by creating legal immigration opportunities. Arrangements that fall outside of the asylum system – such as granting residence permits for people in vocational training or regularisation programmes with cut-off dates – are also ways in which municipalities can achieve greater certainty about the length of time people will be able to stay.

Member states without external EU borders would be responsible for more procedures than at present, but there would be little secondary movement, and member states and their municipalities would know who they were going to receive. Under this proposal, member states would continue to be responsible for returning from municipalities those who are not granted a right to remain. The challenge of determining what happens to people whose asylum requests have been rejected is one that exists everywhere. But it is a problem that can only be exacerbated by accommodating many asylum seekers in one place.

In the short term, municipalities would be responsible for admission and integration/inclusion, and member states would be responsible for asylum procedures and, if necessary, returns. In the medium term, asylum procedures and returns could increasingly be dealt with on a European level and reception and relocation financed entirely from EU funds.

4 | Does that mean that everyone from Africa will come to Europe?

4.1 A humane refugee policy requires a change of perspective: where do Europe's legitimate long-term interests lie?

The key points being put forward here for a humane European asylum and immigration regime will appear to some as if Europe would thus be opening its doors to all the world's refugees, and in particular to those from Africa, thus hopelessly overburdening itself and its own population. If you attempt to identify a humane refugee policy, you will soon be confronted with the question: "Do you really want to open the floodgates? Given their birth rate and unemployment levels, millions of African refugees will come to Europe!"

Since 2015 the perception that the image of an economically attractive Europe has become the main reason that people – and Africans in particular – flee their homelands has gained traction, and not only in Germany. According to this view, they would come in droves if access to Europe were not blocked by forbidding deserts, deadly Mediterranean crossings and an insurmountable Balkan route. In a report published by *Die Zeit*, a department head at Germany's Ministry of the Interior, Helmut Teichmann, stated: "In Niger, each woman has on average more than seven children. The continent's population is exploding." That is one reason, Teichmann says, why more Africans will set off for Europe in the future, regardless of how dangerous the crossing may be: "As long as the door is open, even if only by a crack, they will carry on trying."[1] The more

---

1 Friederichs, H., and C. Lobenstein (2016) "Die gekaufte Grenze. Deutschland rüstet afrikanische Staaten wie Tunesien mit Überwachungstechnik auf, um Flüchtlinge zu stoppen. Für europäische Konzerne ist das ein Milliardengeschäft". *Die Zeit* 45/2016, 27 October (www.zeit.de/2016/45/fluechtlinge-grenze-schutz-tunesien-ueberwachungs technik).

---

humane our refugee policy, the greater the so-called pull factor – so say the sceptics and the opponents of a change to a more humane policy. This is the commonly encountered "argument".

The pull factor is in contrast to the push factor, which, instead of attracting refugees or migrants from a distance, repels them from their home country. According to this theory, refugees are fleeing because, for a variety of reasons, they think they have no prospects in their home country. The theory of the pull factor, on the other hand, assumes that the people who flee from their home country undertake the journey because they see a flourishing Europe that tempts them to leave their homelands. This refers not only to those economic migrants that many European states have created access routes for because they need them. Or, to put it another way, the followers of the pull theory actually consider there to be very few genuine refugees, believing that the vast majority who come to Europe are "economic refugees" who want to make a better life for themselves in Europe (at our expense).

Under pressure from national interior ministers in particular, the EU's refugee policy has for years been based on the premise of the predominant importance of the pull factor. Both in principle and in practice, this policy is being pursued in an ever harsher, more restrictive manner, with the aim of preventing the influx of refugees into Europe wherever possible. The main means of warding them off are deterrence and closing borders as tightly as possible. In this view, the doors to Europe must remain shut; the more difficult and dangerous access to Europe is, the better. While such a policy might cost many lives, this view – whether stated explicitly or implicitly – considers there to be no alternative that could save Europe from an influx of refugees. The unspoken vision behind this is a supposedly uncontaminated Europe with its traditionally predominantly white indigenous population, sealing itself off as far as possible against migrants from Africa and the Middle and Far East.

This ignores the increasing numbers of workers from all around world who are welcomed because Germany and the EU need them to fuel their continued economic growth, as Europe's demographic trends indicate a considerable shrinking and, above all, an ageing of its native population. If nothing is done to counteract this, the EU will be considerably weakened in many respects, both economically and in its position and importance in the world.

As a result, many countries have passed laws to facilitate immigration in recent years, including Germany, whose ruling conservative party had laboriously opposed such a law for decades, claiming that Germany was "not a country of immigration". Far-sighted, open-minded figures such as Rita Süssmuth – the former president of the Bundestag – were criticised by Chancellor Angela Merkel as "damaging to the party" at the beginning of the millennium. This was because Süssmuth – a member of Merkel's Christian Democrats and chair of an interparty immigration committee with Jochen Vogel as her deputy, under Chancellor Schroeder's red–green coalition – had elaborated sound foundations for a consensual, interparty German immigration policy.

Ever since the financial crisis of 2007–2009, the German government and, under heavy pressure from Germany, the EU have continued to follow Chancellor Merkel's motto of "proceeding cautiously". This motto suggests meticulousness, security and trustworthiness, and for a good fifteen years it has made the Germans grow accustomed to a provincial short-sightedness that, on the basis of their strong economic position, seem to have no need to take account of European or global challenges, nor the needs of their neighbours. They have thus followed the logic described by Karl Deutsch. Deutsch – who fled Prague in the late 1930s following the Nazi invasion of the Sudetenland and went on to become a professor at Harvard – defined power early on in his career as "the ability to afford not to learn".[2] This is the quintessence of the arrogance of power and thus also of short-sightedness.

The principle of short-sightedness in the guise of "prudence" has caused considerable damage, destroyed solidarity and evidently harmed our long-term interests over the years. A prime example of this was the way in which the German government and its finance minister, Wolfgang Schäuble, dealt with the despised Syriza government in Athens in 2015. For the sake of a dogmatic austerity policy and with the aim of educating the "reckless" Greeks (and also to humiliate them because of their debts), Schäuble forced the Greek government to "privatise" the remainder of the port of Piraeus (aside from the cargo side, which already belonged to the Chinese) so that they could pay down public debts from the proceeds. This was an unrealistic objective and hence was absurd.

Despite what the then Greek finance minister, Yanis Varoufakis, had calculated together with a Munich consulting company in order to preserve this strategically important public infrastructure for the Greek state, the entire port was sold to Beijing for next to nothing, which gave China strategic sea access to Europe. A curious form of privatisation. Seven

---

2   Deutsch, K. W. (1969) *Politische Kybernetik: Modelle und Perspektiven* (Freiburg im Breisgau: Rombach), p. 171.

years later, many Europeans have now woken up and are scratching their heads over China's aggressive and strategically driven influence all over the world, including in Europe. We were short-sighted enough to open the door to them. "Proceeding cautiously" has damaged and continues to damage our long-term interests.

This is also the case in Africa: many people have noticed that China has been actively investing, lending and creating dependencies there for years. Many Africans, too, are sceptical about the way that China, under the pretence of "solidarity" with the Global South, and supposedly unlike the arrogant colonial West, is making African countries strategically and systematically dependent. The EU now has the chance to turn over a new leaf and take over from China as Africa's priority partner.

The EU nevertheless believes it can afford to increasingly and overtly exploit its current power imbalance over Africa in its refugee policy while hiding behind the slogans of "partnership with Africa" – of allegedly working together as partners – in order to instrumentalise Africa to the continent's disadvantage but to the benefit of Europe's short-sighted interests. This is something I will come back to. The answer to the question of whether a humane refugee policy would open the door for African refugees to come to Europe therefore requires us not to close the borders without careful consideration. Instead, we need to step back and look more closely at current and potential global developments, as this will enable us to identify our own long-term interests in Africa, a continent in which significant changes in the balance of power have taken place since the last century that will also impact our future way of life. The EU finds itself confronted with major powers – the United States, Russia and China – of which China in particular is clearly pursuing not only economic and systemic interests but also political power in a strategic and consistent manner. They are clearly opposed to our ideas of democracy, the rule of law, power sharing and prosperity in an open society with freedom, justice and solidarity.

If we do not demonstrate in our treatment of Africa the values that characterise our way of life, then we refute in practice what we proclaim morally and demand of others. That makes us appear ever-less credible, acting solely in the interests of our narrow-minded but poorly understood long-term interests and without respect for Africa. By doing so, we are effectively destroying our own future. The more we lose potential and essential partners for a global policy in which our liberal, constitutional and socially responsible way of life can survive and thrive, the more that way of life is lost in moral self-contradiction.

But this is something that is in our own hands! The more we allow ourselves to pursue an idiotic policy of excluding the Global South and thus undermining its development, the more we harm our own future. Perhaps some European governments that are pushing this narrow-minded strategy may thus boost their chances of remaining in government for the next few years, and their heads of government may well be contemplating retirement by the time that that term in office comes to an end – but we and our children will scratch our heads in confusion when we wake up in a world where our opinions no longer matter and we are powerless because we have blackmailed and displayed arrogance instead of cooperation and fellowship towards our neighbours in the Global South and, in particular, in Africa. Our partners have long perceived this to be the case and are seeking alternatives.

We can only give a sound initial answer to the question of whether we want to bring all African refugees to Europe if we at long last adopt a far-sighted perspective that makes our long-term interests clear. Experience has shown that these, unlike our short-term interests, are in line with our values. Only by looking at the world and our political partners with fresh eyes can the migration that characterises our century be shaped in such a way that we achieve reasonably peaceful coexistence not only in Europe and Africa but also in the Middle and Far East – indeed, at a global level.

4.2 Taking a close look at Africa

We must also at long last take a close look at developments in Africa. European refugee policy perceives Africa as a single continent: foreign, hostile, and offering no prospect of identifying common political interests and cooperating in the interests of both parties. Africa is not yet viewed as a politically, culturally, geographically and socially extremely diverse and, at the same time, rich continent, which is exactly the view we need to take if we are to find a viable solution. A humane European refugee and asylum policy must be integrated into a differentiated immigration policy.

The mantra of the European practitioners of the policy of exclusion – that they want to "tackle the causes of migration" in Africa and thus prevent Africans from coming to Europe in the first place – is proof that they are not looking closely. The causes of migration are extremely complex and cannot be solved quickly and easily by, for example, boosting private investment (which is normally the first idea to be mentioned), nor are there any immediate solutions to population displacements. It also fails to show decency and sensitivity on our part; on the contrary, it reflects badly on our own European priorities if we stick to the belief that the most effective incentives for Africa are money and economic prosperity. Africans, just like anyone else, do not live on bread alone.

Of course, ensuring economic subsistence, fighting hunger and unemployment and providing sufficient housing are important, but so are many other things: security against war and political arbitrariness, social safeguards, social networks and affiliations, and also equitable economic prospects in a society not split between rich and poor. It is worth remembering the French sociologist and political philosopher Alexis de Tocqueville in this regard. A politician and writer who focused on the concept of equality, he pointed out that, as overall equality increased, lesser inequalities provoked ever more discord. Karl Marx called this "relative misery". We Europeans still often believe that it is only absolute misery that can be avoided or overcome, that Africans need only a roof over their heads and enough to eat to be satisfied with their lives in their homelands, and that they have no right to demand more. This view is the ultimate in arrogance.

Africans are well aware of whether Europeans really take them seriously as partners in determining their own way of life, desires and needs or whether they want to determine from above what should be sufficient for Africans, concentrating only on European interests.

A treasure trove of insights into these connections and empirical findings is provided by the 2020 annual report compiled by the Expert Council on Integration and Migration (Sachverständigenrat deutscher Stiftungen für Integration und Migration; SVR) under the title "A Joint Endeavour: Shaping Migration from Africa to Europe".[3]

This detailed report is an extremely valuable source of insights on what has been going on for years in the relationship between Europe and Africa – some of it good, but most of it bad and increasingly so. At the same time, it shows the opportunities to help shape Africa that we would have if we were to engage with the continent and its people, given its energy and internal diversity and the many cultural, material, psychological, economic and political factors behind migration from Africa. As stated in the summary of the expert report, our decisive principle of action should be that "states and partnerships of states such as the EU should try to shape the framework conditions for migration in a way that

---

3 Expert Council on Integration and Migration (2020) "Gemeinsam gestalten: Migration aus Afrika nach Europa". Annual report (www.svr-migration.de/publikation/jahresgutach ten-2020/).

recognises the interests of countries of origin and destination as well as the needs of migrants themselves".[4]

That is not currently the case, however. Despite the European rhetoric of partnership, the interests of African states and people are increasingly ignored. The EU's objective – which is being forcefully promoted as a matter of priority and even comes with sanctions that would withdraw development aid – is to "externalise" Europe's exclusion of Africans, that is, to transfer it to the African continent. This directly undermines the interests of African states and economic alliances. In order to block migration routes, some of which are centuries old, borders between states are being erected and fortified at great expense. But these have not developed historically; they have been arbitrarily imposed by the colonial powers in accordance with their interests of power and domination.

The West African economic alliance ECOWAS (Economic Community of West African States) – which aims to open borders and promote mobility in order to boost the economy, as Europeans have done on their own continent – is being undermined by Europe. Europeans are impeding the economically reasonable demands of Africans by erecting borders between African states. In doing so, they undermine Africa's independent development and create new reasons for displacement. This is not only a moral but also a serious political self-contradiction on the part of Europeans and another example of their short-sighted policies, which are geared to their own domestic electoral prospects rather than the challenges of global development. Borders play a different historical and cultural role in Africa than in European nation states: "In many African countries, for example, cross-border mobility is taken for granted and is viewed as a natural part of everyday life or individual lifestyle."[5] The EU, however, does not consider it necessary to take the historical and cultural roots of African societies seriously and to adapt to them.

This shows a lack of respect for Africa. In addition to blocking migration routes, the European Union is increasingly emphasising deportations to Africa and corresponding agreements with African states as a second focus of its refugee policy, although the numbers of those deported are small compared with the actual numbers migrating. Nonetheless, the EU – erroneously – expects this to have a deterrent effect on potential refugees. It also believes that the established European population set great store by this policy, and that they would lose confidence in their

---

4   Ibid., p. 10.

5   Ibid., p. 15.

governments if they were seen to be avoiding legally required deportations. But though in principle compliance with the law is, of course, a prerequisite for the rule of law, laws that cause harm to politics in the long term are counterproductive and must be changed.

We in Europe also fail to take into account that deportations are perceived in Africa as a humiliation by the people deported, the countries taking them back and those people's family members or fellow town or village residents who financed their journey. This is why African governments generally keep such deals with Europe discreet and informal, agreeing on procedures that their societies are kept unaware of as much as possible, in order to ensure that they do not turn against their governments.

Tangible interests also speak out against deportation back to the African country of origin: the remittances that migrants send back from Europe are often very important for family members at home and for the economy, amounting to more than the funds received from European or national development cooperation aid and now far exceeding the offers made by Europeans to buy the compliance of those African countries.

In many African countries, the causes of displacement and migration include violence, authoritarian or dictatorial rule, and insecurity – in other words, not only economic but also political problems. Europeans repeatedly counter the interests of African societies by cooperating with autocratic rulers and creating new reasons for migration.[6] The large surges in involuntary migration from Africa are the consequences of dangerous political conflicts and civil wars.[7]

Moreover, the EU often deprives Africans of their livelihoods through its own activities. Off the coasts of West Africa in particular, European (and also, for example, Chinese) fishing fleets are emptying the seas and robbing the population of their main source of food. Unfair treaties between West African governments and the EU mean that such occurrences are not infrequent. Civil society initiatives are important sources of assistance in this regard. They ensure transparency in the flow of money between African governments and the companies with fish factories situated just a few miles off the African coast, and they help prevent corruption, a major cause of problems that originates from both developed

---

6   See Koch, A., A. Weber and I. Werenfels (eds) (2018) "Profiteers of migration? Authoritarian states in Africa and European migration management". SWP Research Paper 4. German Institute for International and Security Affairs, July.

7   For a detailed account, see Expert Commission on the Causes of Flight (2021) "Krisen vorbeugen, Perspektiven schaffen, Menschen schützen".

countries and African governments. These organisations include, for example, the Fisheries Transparency Initiative (FiTI), which was officially established in 2019. Exports of subsidised European foodstuffs to Africa also harm our neighbours' food production.[8]

Overall, the European Union is increasingly aligning its Africa policy towards only two objectives: reducing irregular migration and deporting Africans back to Africa – set against the background of a deterrence policy whose promotion of partnership is no more than an empty phrase. The Expert Council on Integration and Migration therefore concludes:

> It is a strategic necessity for the EU [...] to focus more on African interests in the future if it is to take a genuinely cooperative approach to reducing irregular migration, while striking a balance within migration policy.[9]

It is not as moral indictment that I cite the various reasons for the migration of Africans, in which the EU is also causally implicated, and the EU's humiliating displays of superiority. Of course, such indictment would be justified. My prime concern, however, is to show that we have much more scope for shaping our relationship with the various African countries and, above all, with the people in the cities and municipalities (which is something I will return to) than is generally acknowledged in public discourse. We have significantly more options in our hands than trying to tackle a century-long history of migration by means of rigorous exclusion measures. Not only do these fail to stem it, they actually increase it by multiplying its causes. Our exclusion measures give rise only to high moral and political costs and, last but not least, billions of dollars in financial costs. We could use this enormous amount of money more constructively. Our Africa policy undermines our long-term interests.

Whether the countries of Africa prosper in such a way that people no longer feel compelled to flee, or whether we motivate them to remain in even greater numbers through our policy of isolation, the outcome will depend in large part on our foresight, our imagination, our openness to the world and our diplomatic skills – in short, on whether we are prepared to acknowledge that we live in *one* world, in which we can achieve much more by working together than against each other.

Instead of erecting borders within Africa against the will of Africans, instead of blackmailing them with the threat of cutting off development

---

8   Expert Council on Integration and Migration (2020) "Gemeinsam gestalten", pp. 54, 97.
9   Ibid., p. 133.

aid or buying the goodwill of governments against the interests of the people, instead of depleting their fishing grounds and reducing the value of the food they produce with imports of subsidised European food, instead of cooperating with and legitimising autocrats and thus contributing to the lack of prospects for people under their rule, instead of denying Africans legal ways to access Europe, such as offering their youth a well-rounded education that extends beyond only academic education, we can negotiate in our own interests on an eye-to-eye basis about where they see their interests and how we can reconcile them with ours. That would be truly acting in Europe's long-term interests.

In the 1980s Willy Brandt and the Brundtland report far-sightedly pioneered the promulgation of the goal of sustainability and the "joint development" of North and South. Working towards this goal would certainly not put an end to labour migration – which is something Europeans themselves have an interest in – but it would enable it to be shaped and promoted.

4.3 Challenges and opportunities of development cooperation with Africa

Even if we undertake the necessary change of perspective – and switch our policy from self-destructive deterrence to intelligent cooperation and a reconciliation of interests with Africa, and finally start to devise policy with confidence in ourselves and the future rather than on the basis of fear – a common future will still not simply fall into our laps. In reality, there are of course an infinite number of conflicting interests. There are dilemmas to face, as current research on Africa shows, such as the fact that migration tends to be initially encouraged by economic development in African countries and that the emigration rate only begins to decrease after a further stage of development (the "migration hump").[10] This finding is plausible because overcoming absolute poverty is what makes migration possible in the first place, allowing people to make comparisons and decide that they would be better off somewhere else.

Maintaining absolute poverty wherever possible cannot be the answer. Instead, we must promote and accelerate the next stage of development, which would in turn make staying more attractive. If we measure our relationship with Africa and migration solely in terms of whether migration declines or stops, we force ourselves into a stalemate. Instead, we

---

10   Ibid., p. 54.

need an idea of common "sustainable development", as provided for in the 2030 sustainability goals to which the EU is, after all, officially fully committed.

This fundamental change of perspective is therefore a necessary but not sufficient condition for a relationship between Europe and Africa that would benefit both parties and overcome the concerns that a humane European refugee policy would expose Europe to an unmanageable "flood" of African refugees. What is needed are political decisions as part of a broader strategy towards Africa – decisions that help our neighbours in the South achieve sustainable development and that also provide them with tangible assistance when they assume tasks on behalf of us and others, particularly around migration.

For example, few people outside the African continent realise that some African countries are themselves host countries (such as Ethiopia for refugees from the Horn of Africa) and that they receive particularly large numbers of refugees from intra-African migration (such as Uganda receiving those from Sudan). To prevent these host countries, which are much poorer than us, from suffering serious damage to their own development as a result of their hosting activities – damage that would also lead to more emigration to Europe – it would make sense for the EU to support them and to thus enable refugees to stay close to their home countries, as they themselves wish to do.

As the Expert Council on Integration and Migration has stated:

Some of the biggest refugee camps in the world are situated in Africa. This includes the refugee settlement of Bidi with some 231,400 inhabitants in the northwest of Uganda (as of January 2020 [...]),[11] the Dadaab camp complex with some 218,800 (as of July 2020 [...])[12] and the Kakuma camp with some 153,600 people in Kenya (as of August 2019 [...])[13] and the Nyarugusu camp with some 136,550 people in Tanzania (as of January 2020 [...]).[14]

Refugee camps are generally designed only for temporary accommodation, but the reality is often different and protracted situations are becoming increasingly

---

11   "Refugees and asylum-seekers in Uganda: Uganda refugee response". UNHCR website, January 2020 (https://data2.unhcr.org/en/documents/details/73905).

12   "Dadaab refugee complex". UNHCR Kenya website (www.UNHCR.org/ke/Dadaab-refugee-complex).

13   "Population statistics per location: Kakuma Camp". UNCHR website, 31 August 2019 (https://data2.unhcr.org/en/documents/download/71190).

14   "Tanzania: refugee situation statistical report". UNCHR website, 31 January 2020 (https://data2.unhcr.org/en/documents/details/74028).

prevalent. These are situations in which at least 25,000 refugees of a nationality have been living in exile in a host country for more than five years.[15]

The European Union could also help financially to ensure that the large refugee camps that have existed in Africa for decades do not remain "foreign bodies" in their host countries indefinitely. There are already attempts to offer their residents better opportunities for integrating into the host country, and to convert the camps into new, truly functioning cities. Some of these are already underway. One of the biggest challenges is the anticipated youth unemployment in Africa resulting from the expected population increase. Training young people on temporary stays in Europe, enabling microloans and preventing the brain drain to Europe are all measures that could assist the African states.

For many Africans, seasonal work in Europe is the order of the day. This could be ameliorated by temporary European work visas. The Expert Council on Integration and Migration has proposed that these could require a deposit that would be repaid when Africans returned to their home country. Such a return would then not be humiliating. As its report states:

> For many African countries, especially in view of their demographic profile, allowing entry for the purposes of completing an apprenticeship could be of relevance. And with the possibility of re-entering to take subsequent qualifications, which provides projects at the interface of development and migration policy – such as the "Triple Win" policy – with their own legal basis, migration policy activities could be specifically developed and promoted in countries that are particularly suitable for reasons of development, foreign policy and migration policy.[16]

One obstacle to the effectiveness of development cooperation between Europe and Africa is that its orientation and concrete implementation are in the hands of national governments in both continents. An exception in this regard is the contribution of the very many NGOs in both the North and the South, which provide indispensable services. As in the EU, Africa's national governments are rarely the political actors that drive forward developments with determination and innovation.

The fight against the pandemic has shown that such actors are more likely to be found at the local level. Similarly, "wherever mayors and

---

15   Expert Council on Integration and Migration (2020) "Gemeinsam gestalten", p. 136.
16   Ibid., p. 103. See also Expert Commission on the Causes of Flight (2021), p. 130 ff.

regional councils quickly assumed responsibility during the Ebola crisis in 2014, the disease was rapidly contained."[17] As in Europe, this also opens up opportunities for people to participate at the local level in a way that is effective and relevant to their lives. This is the place to test and further develop good-governance practices from the bottom up – transparent decision-making, fair participation and interactions with one another, discussion of citizens' ideas, a sense of responsibility and practicality – and to link these to people's lifestyles, experiences and capacities.

Our national development policies often rely primarily on providing funding through extensive government programmes and projects, as well as major government initiatives, but often they do not take into account the need to combine financial investments with sound administration and democratic participation in order to make them sustainable. Large-scale government investment is nevertheless still needed, although it can open the door to corruption. This could be prevented by good-governance regulations, or by well-formulated integrity pacts, for which Transparency International has made good proposals.

A strategy of local development cooperation between European and African municipalities and cities could lead to a new political impetus towards shared sustainable development. Many relevant initiatives and reference points already exist. It is no coincidence that cities and communities are particularly open and capable of sustainable development cooperation. In other words, we are returning to the basis of our proposal for a humane European refugee and migration policy in cooperation with Africa.

4.4 Fresh momentum: development cooperation between African and European municipalities

An example of cooperation between Libyan and European cities: the Nicosia Initiative
Following the death of Libya's ruler Muammar Gaddafi in 2011 and the collapse of its centralised dictatorial structure, cities and municipalities became new anchors of social cohesion amid the country's chaos. In 2012 they were given the political responsibility of administering themselves for the first time. In the extreme uncertainty of a

17 Starzmann, P. (2020) "Wie afrikanische Politiker in der Coronakrise alte Klischees widerlegen". *Der Tagesspiegel*, 11 May (www.tagesspiegel.de/politik/ewiger-krisenkon tinent-wie-afrikanische-politiker-in-der-coronakrise-alte-klischees-widerlegen/25819236. html).

society without a central government, the elected municipal assemblies became the places where confidence could be rebuilt.[18]

Against this background, the EU's Committee of the Regions invited Libyan mayors seeking experience and expertise in local self-government to a meeting with European mayors. This resulted in the so-called Nicosia Initiative. Benedetta Oddo – a political consultant who managed social responsibility initiatives in Libya, both in development cooperation and in the private sector, and who was primarily involved in local self-government – helped bring together a network of Libyan and European cities. For Libya, these included Sirte, Tripoli, Gharyan and Zintan in the west; Sebha in the south; and Benghazi and Tobruk in the east. The European side involved the Belgian city of Antwerp, the Portuguese city of Vila Real, the Spanish city of Murcia, the Cypriot capital Nicosia, the Belgian region of Flanders and the Maltese local authorities. The subjects of the cooperation were water management, waste management, primary healthcare, public administration and municipal budgets.

In 2016, Federica Mogherini, then the EU's High Representative for Foreign Affairs and Security Policy, met with the Committee of the Regions and representatives of the Nicosia Initiative and praised the latter as an important example of urban diplomacy, which she defined as a global strategy of local action. This role of the local level within the framework of a global sustainable development strategy can serve as a model for a strategy of shared sustainable development for the European Union and Africa. At the EU level, the Committee of the Regions should be supported in its current activities and play a much larger role than it has in the past.

Several researchers have recently produced valuable studies on this topic under the auspices of the German Institute of International and Security Affairs.[19] This research highlights how cooperation between African and European cities and city networks could lead to joint sustainable development that would in turn benefit a humane refugee policy and

---

18 El Kamouni-Janssen, F., H. Shadeedi and N. Ezzeddine (2018) "Local security governance in Libya: perceptions of security and protection in a fragmented country". Report. Clingendael Netherlands Institute for International Relations (www.clingendael. org/pub/2018/diversity_security_Libya/).

19 See, for example, Angenendt, S., N. Biehler and D. Kipp (2021) "Cities and their networks in EU–Africa migration policy: are they really game changers?" SWP Research Paper 8. German Institute for International and Security Affairs, November.

a positive shaping of migration. This reminds us of how the previously struggling German Covid-19 vaccination campaign saw a surge in vaccinations in April 2021 after general practitioners were given permission to administer the vaccine. The many decentralised vaccination options led the daily vaccination rates to double overnight from around 350,000 to around 700,000, which highlights the effectiveness and dynamics of decentralised initiatives.

At the same time, this research identifies the current obstacles that are impeding the enormous potential of municipal cooperation.

As with Europe's refugee policy, one of the obstacles is that local authorities in cities and municipalities have insufficient financing and staff to undertake such cooperation, a role that until now has been reserved for national governments, which generally obstruct each other's proposals. National governments on both continents zealously safeguard their power, even at the expense of actually finding solutions. That comes as no surprise, as national governments are under no pressure to solve these problems.

If there is to be a renewed impetus in the joint development of Africa and Europe, it is therefore crucial that cities and municipalities are given sufficient funding and scope to act and that national governments cooperate with them. There is no reason this cannot be done. In this context, research repeatedly refers to the exemplary nature of German municipal self-government.[20]

In addition to the lack of funding, the diversity of cities and their all-consuming day-to-day problems make it difficult for them to coordinate refugee and migration policies, and to push tenaciously for the implementation of their political strategies and the achievement of their goals.

On the other hand, the potential offered by municipal cooperation, the urgency of the task and the fact that municipal-level approaches are perceived worldwide as a promising way to solve pressing local and global problems are all becoming increasingly apparent.

The number of community initiatives and networks worldwide was estimated at around 200 in 2016. It is difficult to summarise them clearly. Angenendt et al. create an overview of sorts with the following classification:

---

20   See the book by the administrative lawyer and former ombudsperson Irena Lipowicz, published in Poland in 2019 (pp. 39 ff). Irena Lipowicz also attests to the Polish roots of self-government.

City networks can be differentiated by their profile: generalist ones such as Euro-cities;[21] thematic ones, such as Polis for traffic in Europe or Platforma[22] for development cooperation; and geographical ones such as the Union of Baltic Cities[23] or MedCities.[24] There are also linguistic-cultural networks, often aligned with (former) colonial structures, such as the Commonwealth Local Government Forum[25] or Association Internationale des Maires Francophones;[26] multi-stakeholder networks such as the Cities Alliance; networks brought into being by philanthropical foundations, for example C40; or those established on individual initiatives, such as the Global Parliament of Mayors.[27]

Refugee policy and migration have not, to date, been among their priorities, but they are clearly becoming increasingly important, and the EU now also supports the activities of cities and municipalities in this regard, which means that there are points of reference here for a humane European refugee policy.

In February 2019, for example, the European Commission, together with the Committee of the Regions, organised the Cities and Regions for Development Cooperation Forum, inviting local and regional authorities from Europe and partners from elsewhere, including Africa.[28] In 2018, 150 city representatives met in Marrakesh and undertook to implement the UN's Global Compact for Migration. The Mayoral Forum on Human Mobility, Migration and Development, which has been in existence since 2014, had already committed itself to this goal, and since 2020 the mayoral forum and the Global Forum on Migration and Development have been working together on this issue.[29] They are financially supported by the Swiss Agency for Development and Cooperation, the Open Society Foundations and the Robert Bosch Foundation. As can be seen, public financing is lacking.

---

21   See https://eurocities.eu.

22   See https://platforma-dev.eu.

23   See www.ubc.net.

24   See www.medcities.org.

25   See www.clgf.org.uk.

26   See www.aimf.asso.fr.

27   Angenendt et al. (2021) "Cities and their networks in EU–Africa migration policy", p. 22.

28   Ibid, pp. 18–19.

29   Ibid, p. 17.

The EU and national development cooperation policies should and could be creative in their approach to this key question of financing the work of cities and municipalities in the pursuit of a humane refugee and migration policy. An initial experimental step was taken by using the aforementioned EU Emergency Trust Fund to support two municipalities: Koboko in Uganda and Assosa in Ethiopia, both of which have been severely impacted by refugee movements.[30]

Municipal development cooperation offers attractive additional opportunities to tackle the expected increase in African youth unemployment, which I have already mentioned in the context of cooperation between national governments and the EU. The local authorities on both sides have a better understanding of their needs and the potential opportunities and can thus cooperate in a much more focused manner for the benefit of both parties. Training partnerships would be another possibility. Milan's city administration has now launched a project that implements such a partnership with a consortium of partners (Turin city council, the Piedmontese employment agency, local stakeholders in Morocco, and the city of Tunis).[31]

The research group summarises the possibilities as follows:

> There is a role for cities here. If African cities – which are interested in better employment opportunities for their citizens abroad – were systematically included in shaping African-European labour migration, then they could be involved in a meaningful exchange with European cities that have specific labour needs.[32]

The EU's Cities and Regions for Development Cooperation Forum and the Committee of the Regions, like the Africa-Europe Local and Regional Government Forum, have called for support for municipal partnerships between the African Union and the EU, and have demanded far-reaching reforms from the EU to facilitate funding, local financial autonomy and technical support for municipal partnerships.[33]

The authors of the research cite four clear political steps to support municipal development cooperation with Africa:

---

30   Ibid, p. 18.
31   Ibid, p. 20.
32   Ibid., p. 30.
33   Ibid, p. 23–24.

---

(1) designing funding instruments for cities that are more sensitive to migration and forced displacement; (2) facilitating loans for cities by creating new funding instruments so that these cities can better fulfil their tasks in this context; (3) tailoring humanitarian aid more specifically to cities in an emergency – especially the reception of large numbers of forcibly displaced persons; and (4) supporting processes of fiscal decentralisation that make it possible for cities to develop their own financial resources in the long term.[34]

The funding must also take into account what we have already underlined in the section on the decentralised reception of refugees for the EU: mayors must be helped to take in refugees by providing funding not only for refugees but also for the local population, which would remove the rivalry between poor locals and poor refugees and thus the hatred against refugees and migration.

This approach has recently been adopted in Africa in order to offer refugees living in camps the opportunity to integrate into the surrounding society. Uganda has been generous in its reception of refugees from South Sudan, who, for example, receive their own piece of land to work on. Although there already existed a fundamental harmony between locals and refugees, the country has also now made sure that not only refugees but locals too have benefited from new social provisions.[35]

Moreover, in Africa as in Europe, the urban development associated with receiving refugees and organising migration in the broader sense should be made participatory; businesses and organised civil society can play important constructive roles in this process.[36] In this way, joint sustainable development between Europe and Africa in order to humanely manage refugee policy and migration would at the same time strengthen democratic participation and governance on both sides. This, in turn, would be capable of stemming the tide of refugees, including to Europe.

*

The key to supporting local development cooperation between Africa and the EU is to provide direct support to cities and communities and to allocate financial and other services not only through the national level.

Cooperation between European and African cities and municipalities would, after all, also be a humane and intelligent political way to dissuade

---

34 Ibid., p. 24.

35 Expert Council on Integration and Migration (2020) "Gemeinsam gestalten", p. 145.

36 Angenendt et al. (2021) "Cities and their networks in EU–Africa migration policy", p. 26.

African refugees already on migration routes to Europe from embarking on the dangerous journey across the Mediterranean. The EU could provide financial and political support to African communities along the refugee routes so that they in turn could take in refugees and offer them a future. Instead of blocking the established routes and connections, they could support the launching of businesses in the African communities that serve as transit stations, and they could also provide the towns with financial support to settle refugees. This could be done together with North African NGOs, which also have no interest in seeing their compatriots leave for Europe in misery and mortal danger. At the same time, the formation of a participatory infrastructure (multi-stakeholder governance) could be promoted in these municipalities, which would see representatives of municipalities, businesses, and civil society organisations and initiatives work together to further develop their community.

Instead, the EU is increasingly investing billions in Frontex and border protection, in training African police officers and border guards, and, last but not least, in large-scale purchases from the European arms industry, for which tracking down African refugees has become an extremely lucrative business model.[37] These billion-dollar investments in weapons and surveillance equipment do not bring about economic growth.

*

At the beginning of this chapter I asked the question: "Does that mean that everyone from Africa will come to Europe?"

My answer is that, if we recognise our long-term interests, take a closer look at Africa, and do not treat the continent as a black box into which we put all our, often racist, prejudices, we will have much more scope to work towards mutually beneficial cooperation than we might first think. This is not something that will happen of its own accord; it will require imagination, energy, strategic action and courage. Nonetheless, if we act strategically, not "all" Africans will come to Europe, as there will be other, more attractive prospects in their own homelands. Indeed, the vast majority of African refugees currently remain in Africa, as close to their homes as possible.

What the future holds therefore depends to a considerable degree on us Europeans. Our "power" does not lie in drones, weapons and border fences that undermine Africa's future, alienate us from Africans and are in essence very primitive instruments. Instead, our "power", as Hannah

---

37   Friederichs, H., and C. Lobenstein (2016) "Die gekaufte Grenze".

Arendt might put it, lies in our ability to initiate and carry out joint projects, in our ingenuity, our lack of prejudice, our courage and, last but not least, our belief in our values. None of these would be of any use and could be abandoned from the outset if they did not provide a guide for our common survival and development in pursuit of "the good life".

What future does continuing the current refugee policy offer? Or, to put the question more pointedly, what is the price we all pay for continuing Europe's inhumane refugee policy – a policy that is in opposition to our long-term interests?

5 | The costs of "business as usual" and what we are overlooking

By indulging in a delusion of omnipotence and believing that we can totally block refugees from accessing Europe, we are not only acting inhumanely but also depriving ourselves of a common future with Africa, in a world where allies are essential for our way of life.

We are undermining the prosperity of our neighbouring continent, which will in turn increase the number of Africans who will make their way to Europe.

We are also promoting destructive rage and aggression in Africa, which will unleash terrorism that will also affect Europe.

We are pumping huge sums of money into arms companies by funding increasing numbers of weapons, border fortifications, drones and prisons at Europe's external borders and in Africa, instead of using that money for constructive, peaceful solutions.

Our illusory strategy of isolationism has given rise to an undignified dependence on capricious dictators such as Turkey's President Erdoğan, who has only contempt for Europe and its representatives. Not only does he himself act cynically, he also sees through the hypocrisy of the Europeans when they accuse him of disregarding human rights in his country.

We are also losing our respect for ourselves, because we cannot hide forever from our hypocritical approach towards the values we proclaim. Our loss of self-respect goes hand in hand with our loss of self-esteem.

The politicians – who essentially execute this policy in the European Council, against the wishes of the European Parliament – continue these hypocritical double standards and then wonder why the citizenry has lost confidence in their policies and the European Union. They do not understand that the inability to find constructive solutions gives rise to frustration and fear, and that people are unable to live in a schizophrenic state indefinitely, even if the politicians who are responsible for decision-making seem unperturbed by such double standards.

Politicians wishing to retain a certain sense of realism despite this dichotomy – even if merely to keep their feet on the ground – must become clear-sighted cynics who know that the values they proclaim have no bearing on their political decisions. However, they cannot publicly admit to this cynicism, because of the corrosive effect it would have on a democratic society.

As we can see, the cost of the European Union's inhumane refugee policy is overwhelming – but does the threat of high costs motivate people to change their policies? Are warnings and deterrence the only tools we can employ to bring about change? What alternative could we use to attract and convince instead?

*

It would look like this.

We pursue our understanding of our own long-term, sustainable interests, which lie in finding a peaceful, comfortable, positive future in a shared world.

This includes finding constructive ways to deal with migration and displacement, and abandoning the illusion that we in Europe can shut ourselves off.

This also includes understanding migration as an opportunity for all and turning it into a win-win situation instead of constantly putting obstacles in each other's way.

In Europe we can build on the constructive long-term interests of municipalities that are willing to welcome refugees and migrants not just for humanitarian reasons but also to ensure their own future.

We can ensure that their decisions enjoy broad support by setting up "municipal development advisory boards" that will give citizens greater opportunity to participate in developing their living environment in their municipalities.

A "European Fund for Integration and Local Development" can finance both the reception of refugees and, to the same degree, further development in the hosting communities.

Municipalities can place their admission offers on their website, so that refugees and municipalities can reach a consensus of interest via a matching system.

A "coalition of willing states" will mean leaving behind the current deadlock in refugee policy. In consultation with their municipalities willing to receive refugees, they can commit themselves to decentralised refugee reception, including of those who cannot be returned following the completion of their asylum procedure.

Whether conducted in Europe-wide assessment centres or decentralised local ones, European asylum procedures should follow the logic of the Dutch example, prioritising transparency, fairness, trustworthiness and swiftness.

The fear of the "pull factor", particularly around African refugees, can be overcome by constructive joint development with Africa, which in turn brings progress to European and African cities and municipalities.

After all, we have nothing to lose, given the destructive and inhumane refugee policy we currently have.

*

Let us imagine a small town in the European Union, situated in an area that many people leave. There are many such areas in Europe.

Our small town is called Hettstedt. It is located in the southern Harz, in Saxony-Anhalt. Like many other East German towns, Hettstedt lost almost 40% of its population in the years following the fall of the Berlin Wall in 1989, and it has shrunk from about 25,000 inhabitants to only 15,000 today. The mood in the town is one of depression, and its position is imperilled: as its population has decreased, it has seen its financing by the federal state of Saxony-Anhalt (which is calculated per inhabitant) decrease too; maintaining its infrastructure is increasingly expensive given ever fewer inhabitants; and schools and kindergartens have been forced to close. Despite the high level of unemployment, companies are unable to recruit enough workers, apartments stand empty, and the football club can no longer find new young talent. Against this backdrop, Hettstedt's mayor, Danny Kavalier, is looking for solutions.

Together with his administration, he presents the small town's difficult situation to its citizens in a public meeting. Questions are asked about daily life. "Who will care for our old people? How will we recruit teachers for our children, or workers and firefighters?" – this is how the sociologist and economist Andreas Siegert (an expert adviser to the town) will go on to describe their concerns in an interview with the newspaper *Mittel deutsche Zeitung*.[1]

The town has a history that stretches back to the 11th century, in part because of its copper mine. The poet Novalis was born nearby. Hettstedt has picturesque houses, but what it needs are people.

---

1 *Mitteldeutsche Zeitung*, 15 August 2018.

In 2015, a stream of refugees arrive in Germany and the mayor comes up with the idea of receiving more of them than just those allocated to his small town. The majority of residents, including businesses and citizens' initiatives, agree with his idea on condition that they are able to participate in the decision-making – and that is what happens.

The scientific consultant Andreas Siegert and his colleagues conduct interviews: what is important to people?

> It was a question of citizens' satisfaction with the infrastructure, e.g. with local transport, roads, medical care, trade, shopping facilities, culture, sport and social care. We asked what needs to be improved, what people considered to be problems and what makes the place worth living in. We also asked about the economic situation, opportunities for participation and experiences with migrants.[2]

The outcome is interesting:

> Being socially and professionally integrated is very important to people. How much money they earn is often less important. People's first priorities are that their living environment and streets are in good condition. That there are nursery places, schools, parks, social and cultural institutions. It is interesting that the people of Hettstedt are more content overall – despite the town's perceived shortcomings – than those in nearby Eisleben.[3]

Hettstedt takes in refugees and its population stabilises within a few years.

The mayor is supported by the local football club, FC Hettstedt, which had become unable to field a full team and needs young talent. The club makes a significant contribution to ensuring that the new migrant citizens are successfully socially integrated. Its managing director helps find them accommodation and gets the wife of a new player a job with Diakonie, the Protestant social and welfare organisation.

FC Hettstedt now has Syrian, Iraqi and Afghan players. Thanks to the new players and their leading goal scorer, Hussein Alkabib, the club moves up from the region's second division to its premier league, which instils a sense of pride in everyone.[4]

---

2   Ibid.
3   Ibid.
4   *Mitteldeutsche Zeitung*, 13 July 2018.

A Syrian opens a grocery store called Bazaar Palmyra in the town, which sells Arabic delicacies. Its customer base soon extends far beyond the refugee community, as the locals also enjoy the olive salad, the pickled aubergines and the date pastries.

The town works to ensure that there is as much personal interaction as possible between the locals and the refugees. By these means and through cultural projects, people slowly grow to trust each other, which is the basis for all further cooperation.

A theatre project also plays a key role in this regard. The dedicated initiator and director Katrin Schinköth-Haase first conducts geographical and historical "spatial surveys" of the amateur actors she recruits: locals and refugees in Hettstedt between the ages of 6 and 62. They also look for ways to explore their "inner being". People become more involved and write a play together that also deals with the relationships between locals and refugees in Hettstedt. The play is a success that runs to many performances in Hettstedt's packed town hall.[5]

Unfortunately, there is no money for a follow-up project. Yet this is a prime example of how joint cultural activities can bring people together and impart to them new experiences of meaning and understanding, both for the new arrivals and for the established inhabitants.

Hettstedt shows how much better the old and new residents integrate when the newcomers are not simply "forced" onto the locals. As is the case everywhere in Eastern Germany, the AfD is strong in the southern Harz region. There are also violent attacks in the area around Hettstedt – though not in Hettstedt itself.[6]

In this small town in the southern Harz, people discovered how to respond positively to challenging situations with a sense of imagination and energy, and they learned that it is possible to engage meaningfully and enjoy success.

That is precisely what we are missing: the sense of purpose and the joy that come from successful mutual understanding and harmonious coexistence, which we will miss out on if we continue to pursue the current inhumane refugee policy, but which we can enjoy if we work together to develop a humane refugee policy.

---

5 Siegert, A. (ed.) (2019) "'anKommen – willKommen': Regionalkonzept zur Verbesserung der Daseinsvorsorge, Aktivierung Ortsansässiger und nachhaltigen Integration von Einwanderern – Handbuch. Forschungsberichte aus dem zsh 19 – 01". Report. Zentrum für Sozialforschung Halle e.V., p. 72 ff.

6 Ibid., p. 92 ff.

Afterword: what are the consequences of the war in Ukraine for the EU's refugee and migration policy?

The world has changed fundamentally since this book was first published in German in August 2021. The Russian army under President Vladimir Putin has attacked Ukraine and, according to the United Nations, killed tens of thousands of civilians. Millions of Ukrainians have left the country and fled westwards to the European Union – mainly to Poland, but also to Germany and other European countries.

Until Putin's invasion of Ukraine, the EU's refugee and asylum policy was essentially aimed at keeping refugees away from the EU by deterring them – either by condoning pushbacks or carrying them out itself – and by deporting as many people as possible from the EU. In doing so, the EU and its member states have disregarded their values and violated international law on a daily basis.

Immediately after the election in December 2021 of the new federal government of Germany, which in its coalition agreement called for a "new beginning" and a "paradigm shift" in migration policy, the new federal minister of the interior, Nancy Faeser, reached agreement with her French counterpart on the first steps of a fresh start. The new government has so far had little time for a strategic reorientation, of course, because Putin's attack on Ukraine has triggered a tide of refugees unprecedented since World War II. Following several months of war, some 8 million Ukrainians – mainly mothers, children and the elderly – have fled their country. While it is difficult at the moment, reconciling the necessary short-term coordination and measures with long-term strategic steps will be essential.

As with the Syrian war in 2015, the start of the Ukraine war immediately triggered a warm welcome and an enormous wave of sympathy for the refugees. But unlike in 2015, European governments have responded by reactivating the Temporary Protection Directive (sometimes referred to as the "mass influx directive"), which allows refugees to enter EU countries without a visa and receive a protection status with social benefits for one year, which can be extended twice. They are also allowed to work and attend language courses immediately. When the NGO Equal Rights demanded exactly this response in 2015 as a result of the war in Syria, their demand was rejected by the European heads of state and government, including Angela Merkel.

It is interesting that unanimity for this decision on the Temporary Protection Directive was achieved only when it had become clear that refugees would be allowed to move freely within the EU and would not be returned to the EU country of entry – as would have to happen under the Dublin III Regulation. This freedom of movement relies on European citizens organising themselves, both those fleeing and those taking them in, and it allows for flexible responses to the challenge of accommodating them. The overall plan for this reception is, however, currently very uncertain, and this will presumably have to be corrected in the long term.

Something else was also quite different from 2015: Central and Eastern Europe, and Poland in particular, opened its doors to refugees from Ukraine. This was true not only for civil society – much of which had been ready to help refugees previously, which it demonstrated with great commitment by helping those stuck in the deadly trap on the border between Poland and Belarus in early 2022 – but also for the governments of the Visegrád states, which also proved receptive. Viktor Orbán, however, was quick to describe this willingness to help as neighbourly aid rather than refugee aid. Poland continues to be opposed to refugees from the Middle East and is still organising pushbacks against them on its border with Belarus.

Why did the countries of Central and Eastern Europe react very differently in this case than in all previous cases, during which the EU was unable to reach agreement on a humane common refugee policy?

To be sure, important factors in this are the proximity of the Ukrainian war, the fact that it is unambiguously a brutal war of aggression, and the suffering of the Ukrainian people under the attacks of the Russian army, which are broadcast daily on television. In addition, however, there are far more cultural, familial and personal links between Ukrainians and residents of Poland, Hungary, Romania and Moldova than there are between residents of those countries and refugees from the Middle East or Africa. Some 1.5 million Ukrainians were already working in Poland before the war broke out. Many of them had come to Poland after 1989. While they were not entitled to receive any state benefits, there was no question of any problems around integration. Reported cases in which refugees from Ukraine without a Ukrainian passport were rejected at the Polish border, despite the pressing circumstances, were disputed by the Polish government.

The largely positive public climate with regard to the refugees seems to bolster the social pressure against discriminating between those fleeing this terrible conflict situation, since it affects everyone in Ukraine, including Muslim students, for example.

Perhaps this new experience of all the horrors of the Ukraine war will be a learning opportunity for the EU and enable it to agree on a humane refugee policy that would be in its own interests. What could we learn? What will the consequences be?

First, Putin's savage assault on Ukraine, which can be plausibly interpreted as an attack on democracy and the West, teaches us how dependent we Europeans must be on attracting global support and appreciation for democracy if we wish to preserve and enhance our way of life. The fact that in recent years the EU has increasingly used its Africa policy solely to keep African refugees out of Europe has also led Russia and China to strategically expand their influence in Africa via tools such as providing aid for infrastructure development. This highlights the fact that the EU and the West have acted against the interests of African states and peoples, arousing a great deal of aversion and resentment on top of what had already been created by previous experiences of colonialism, as I have pointed before in this book. We need a paradigm shift in the EU's refugee policy if we are to create a global relationship with Africa that is truly based on partnership and that benefits both sides.

Further lessons we could learn from the experiences of the last year are that we can help people under threat of life and limb and that it is best for the EU and for integration if refugees can work and learn German or the language of their host country right from the outset. We could also have greater confidence in the ability of citizens to organise themselves and greatly reduce the internal migration of refugees within the EU by allowing them to choose where they wish to go. We could observe experimentally whether this gives rise to significant governance problems for states and municipalities, or whether the advantages of a voluntary approach and flexibility outweigh any difficulties by avoiding subsequent internal migrations and costly repatriations within the EU.

If we had a practical matching system as described by Malisa Zobel in this book, both urban and rural municipalities – in agreement with national governments – could move quickly to publish the number of refugees they were able to accept on their websites, along with what they could offer them (housing, work, education, health services, transport infrastructure, cultural opportunities, sports, etc.), and could thus attract people who did not want to move to an overcrowded big city. Moreover, experiences gained from occupational integration show that early matching between the wishes and skills of the refugees and the offers of the host countries is very much to the benefit of both sides, and to the employment rate.

There is, of course, a difference between Ukrainian mothers, children and the elderly fleeing from a neighbouring country and young men coming from the Middle East and Africa whom some suspect of being unable or unwilling to integrate into a new and different society. There are also security risks that need to be taken seriously and managed responsibly, which is why the vast majority of Afghans, Syrians, Iraqis, Arabs and Africans who come with good intentions have to endure being viewed with suspicion. We have to be realistic about that and, as a result, the EU cannot simply abandon its visa requirement for everyone.

We can, however, abandon the resentful aversion to refugees and the barely suppressed attitude of envy and competitiveness. A coalition of willing states, as proposed in the agreement reached by Germany's traffic-light coalition government (SPD, FDP and Alliance 90/The Greens) would help to achieve this. In general, there should be less regulation and a more voluntary approach; municipalities, in consultation with their national governments, should be able to play an active role in receiving refugees. Voluntary action could be supported by a European fund that provides financial assistance to municipalities to fund both refugee integration and development not necessarily related to refugees.

This would allow us to act with both compassion and intelligence, a combination that would serve us well in devising a well-thought-out refugee policy.

Bibliography

Angenendt, S., N. Biehler and D. Kipp (2021) "Cities and their networks in EU–Africa migration policy: are they really game changers?" SWP Research Paper 8. German Institute for International and Security Affairs, November.

Bansak, K., J. Ferwerda, J. Hainmueller, A. Dillon, D. Hangartner, D. Lawrence and J. Weinstein (2018) "Improving refugee integration through data-driven algorithmic assignment". *Science*, 359(6373): 325–329.

Bast, J., F. von Harbou and J. Wessels (2020) *Human Rights Challenges to European Migration Policy: The REMAP Study* (Baden-Baden: Nomos).

Calamur, K. (2019) "How technology could revolutionize refugee resettlement". *The Atlantic*, 26 April (www.theatlantic.com/international/archive/2019/04/how-technology-could-revolutionize-refugee-resettlement/587383).

Deutsch, K. W. (1969) *Politische Kybernetik: Modelle und Perspektiven* (Freiburg im Breisgau: Rombach).

El Kamouni-Janssen, F., H. Shadeedi and N. Ezzeddine (2018) "Local security governance in Libya: perceptions of security and protection in a fragmented country". Report. Clingendael Netherlands Institute for International Relations (www.clingendael.org/pub/2018/diversity_security_Libya/).

Expert Commission on the Causes of Flight (2021) "Krisen vorbeugen, Perspektiven schaffen, Menschen schützen". Report of the Federal Government of Germany's Expert Commission on the Causes of Flight (Fachkommission Fluchtursachen).

Expert Council on Integration and Migration (2020) "Gemeinsam gestalten: Migration aus Afrika nach Europa". Annual report (www.svr-migration.de/publikation/jahresgutachten-2020/).

Fontana, S. (2021) "Integrations- & Entwicklungsfonds: Rechtsgutachten zur Umsetzbarkeit einer EU-geförderten kommunalen Integrations- und Entwicklungsinitiative". Friedrich Ebert Stiftung, p. 5 (https://library.fes.de/pdf-files/bueros/bruessel/17884.pdf).

Friederichs, H., and C. Lobenstein (2016) "Die gekaufte Grenze. Deutschland rüstet afrikanische Staaten wie Tunesien mit Überwachungstechnik auf, um Flüchtlinge zu stoppen. Für europäische Konzerne ist das ein Milliardengeschäft". *Die Zeit* 45/2016, 27 October (www.zeit.de/2016/45/fluechtlinge-grenze-schutz-tunesien-ueberwachungstechnik).

Hamilton, A., J. Madison and J. Jay (2009) *The Federalist Papers* (Newhaven, CT: Yale University Press).

Hänsel, V., and B. Kasparek (2020) "Hotspot-Lager als Blaupause für die Reform des Gemeinsamen Europäischen Asylsystems? Politikfolgenabschatzung des Hotspot-Ansatzes in Griechenland". Expert opinion produced on behalf of the Rat für Migration e.V. (Council for Migration), May.

Koch, A., A. Weber and I. Werenfels (eds) (2018) "Profiteers of migration? Authoritarian states in Africa and European migration management". SWP Research Paper 4. German Institute for International and Security Affairs, July.

Lipowicz, I. (2019) *Samorzad Terytorialny XXI Wieku [Territorial Self-Government in the 21st Century]* (Warsaw: Wolters Kluwer).

Lüdke, S. (2020) "UNHCR head on EU refugee policy: 'One of the richest places on earth is failing to get its act together'". *Der Spiegel*, 30 June (www.spiegel.de/ausland/unhcr-chef-filippo-grandi-ueber-fluechtlinge-wenn-uganda-das-schafft-warum-nicht-europa-a-ad9a28b5-3204-4fb2-a733-973c3c698e77).

Mijatović, D. (2020) "Protecting refugees in Europe: the ECHR and beyond". Council of Europe, 22 June (https://rm.coe.int/protecting-refugees-in-europe-the-echr-and-beyond-video-speech-by-dunj/16809ebe73).

Scherrer, A. (2020) "Dublin Regulation on international protection application: European Implementation Assessment". European Parliamentary Research Service (www.europarl.europa.eu/RegData/etudes/STUD/2020/642813/EPRS_STU(2020)642813_EN.pdf).

Schmalz, Dana (2019) "Zur Reichweite von Menschenrechtspflichten: Zugang zu Schutz an den Grenzen Europas". *Newsletter Menschenrechte* (5), 367–376.

Siegert, A. (ed.) (2019) " 'anKommen – willKommen': Regionalkonzept zur Verbesserung der Daseinsvorsorge, Aktivierung Ortsansässiger und nachhaltigen Integration von Einwanderern – Handbuch. Forschungsberichte aus dem zsh 19 – 01". Report. Zentrum für Sozialforschung Halle e.V.

Starzmann, P. (2020) "Wie afrikanische Politiker in der Coronakrise alte Klischees widerlegen". *Der Tagesspiegel*, 11 May (www.tagesspiegel.de/politik/ewiger-krisenkontinent-wie-afrikanische-politiker-in-der-coronakrise-alte-klischees-widerlegen/25819236.html).

Strittmatter, K. (2021) "Dänemark schickt Geflüchtete zurück nach Syrien". *Süddeutsche Zeitung*, 15 April (www.sueddeutsche.de/politik/daenemark-syrien-asyl-fluechtlinge-1.5265844).

Thränhardt, D. (2016) *Asylverfahren in den Niederlanden* (Gütersloh: Bertelsmann Stiftung), p. 12 (www.bertelsmann-stiftung.de/fileadmin/files/Projekte/28_Einwanderung_und_Vielfalt/IB_Studie_ Asylverfahren_NL_Thraenhardt_2016.pdf).

Trapp, A., A. Teytelboym, A. Martinello, T. Andersson and N. Ahani (2020) "Placement optimization in refugee resettlement". Working paper 2018:23. Department of Economics, Lund University (http://project.nek.lu.se/publications/workpap/papers/wp18_23).

Trudeau, J. (2018) "Statement of apology on behalf of the Government of Canada to the passengers of the MS St. Louis". Website of the Prime Minister of Canada, 7 November (https://pm.gc.ca/en/news/speeches/2018/11/07/statement-apology-behalf-government-canada-passengers-ms-st-louis).

UNHCR (2020) "To the European Union: resettlement needs and key priorities for 2021". UNHCR recommendations (www.unhcr.org/en-us/publications/euro series/5fb7e43a4/unhcr-recommendations-european-unionresettlement -needs-key-priorities.html).

Zick, T. (2021) "Schwere Vorwürfe gegen Europas Flüchtlingspolitik". *Süddeutsche Zeitung*, 9 March (www.sueddeutsche.de/politik/migration-mittelmeer -europa-menschenrechte-1.5229226).

About the author

Dr Gesine Schwan is president of the Berlin Governance Platform (formerly HUMBOLDT-VIADRINA Governance Platform), former professor of political sciences at the Free University of Berlin, and chair of the SPD Commission for Basic Values.